Your First Year as an Elementary Music Teacher

Your First Year as an Elementary Music Teacher

A Practical Guide for New Educators

Andrew S. Paney

OXFORD
UNIVERSITY PRESS

Oxford University Press is a department of the University of Oxford. It furthers the University's objective of excellence in research, scholarship, and education by publishing worldwide. Oxford is a registered trade mark of Oxford University Press in the UK and certain other countries.

Published in the United States of America by Oxford University Press
198 Madison Avenue, New York, NY 10016, United States of America.

Library of Congress Cataloging-in-Publication Data
Names: Paney, Andrew S., author.
Title: Your first year as an elementary music teacher : a practical guide for new educators / Andrew S. Paney.
Description: New York, NY : Oxford University Press, 2025. |
Includes bibliographical references and index.
Identifiers: LCCN 2025002495 (print) | LCCN 2025002496 (ebook) | ISBN 9780197631447 (paperback) | ISBN 9780197631430 (hardback) | ISBN 9780197631461 (epub)
Subjects: LCSH: Music teachers—Training of. | Music—Instruction and study. | Music—Instruction and study—Outlines, syllabi, etc. | LCGFT: Lesson plans.
Classification: LCC MT1.P255 Y68 2025 (print) | LCC MT1.P255 (ebook) |
DDC 780.71—dc23/eng/20250129
LC record available at https://lccn.loc.gov/2025002495
LC ebook record available at https://lccn.loc.gov/2025002496

DOI: 10.1093/oso/9780197631430.001.0001

Paperback printed by Marquis Book Printing, Canada
Hardback printed by Bridgeport National Bindery, Inc., United States of America

The manufacturer's authorized representative in the EU for product safety is Oxford University Press España S.A., Parque Empresarial San Fernando de Henares, Avenida de Castilla, 2 – 28830 Madrid (www.oup.es/en).

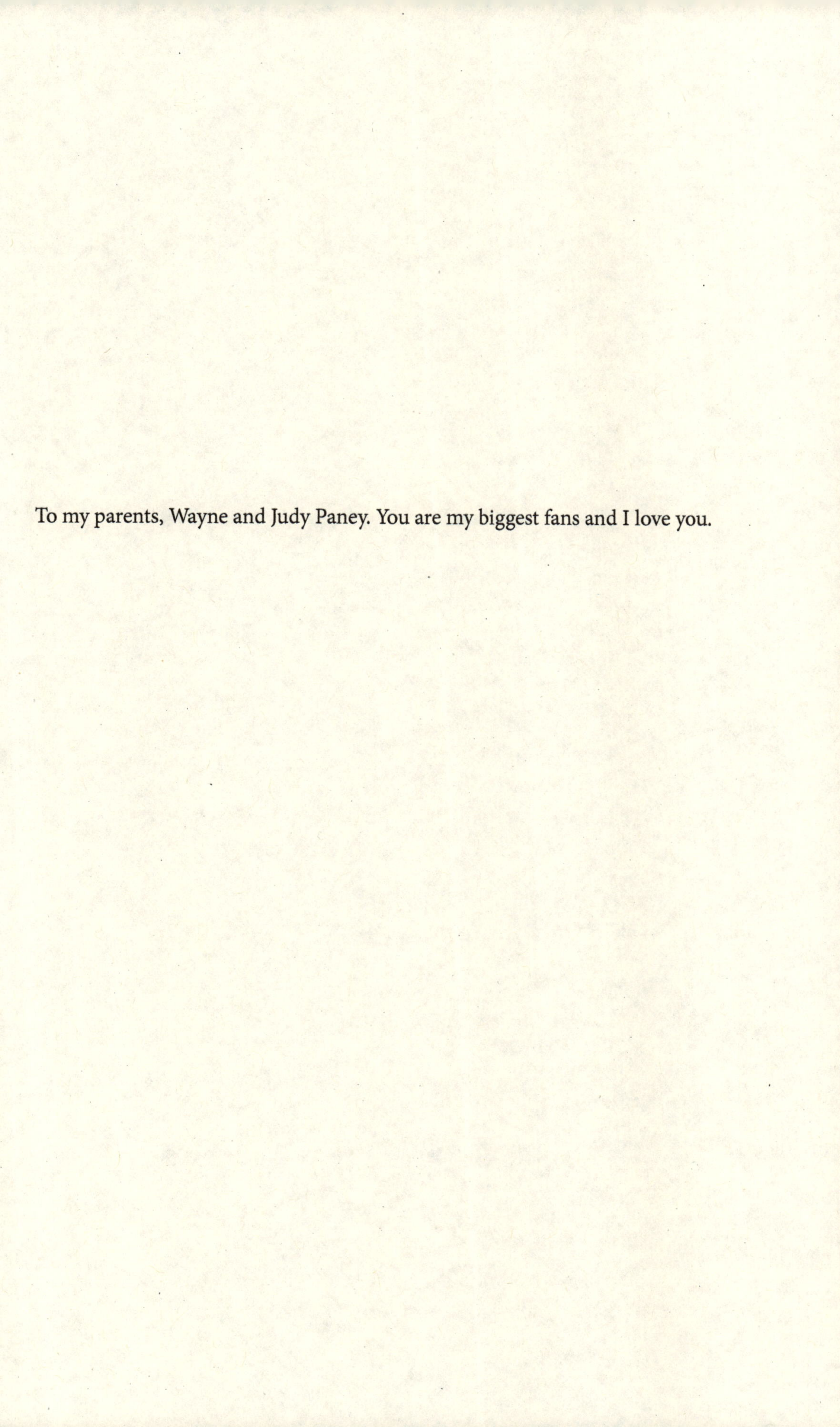

To my parents, Wayne and Judy Paney. You are my biggest fans and I love you.

Contents

Figures

Acknowledgments

I am especially grateful to my musical and academic mentors who saw potential in me and encouraged me to keep going. Alan Spurgeon, you helped me become a happy music scholar. Susan Brumfield, you inspire me with your magical teaching skills. Jan Killian, I try to emulate your positive, encouraging approach to new researchers and scholars. Jean Ellsworth, when I was hungry for and desperate for the beauty of music, you opened my ears and modeled using music to serve the Lord and people. To the late Curtis Funk, you saw I could be a good teacher and helped me see it, too.

Some dear friends, all excellent teachers, read my work and improved it. Amanda Johnston, you gave great tips for writing the book proposal (and asking for an extension!). Alice Hammel, you cheered me on and made me smile. Sandy Knudson, you love children and learning and I'm glad to have you on my team. Ramon Jackson, your optimism and commitment to students' learning makes me a better teacher. Susan and Don Garrett, how generous you are to me and others in our region. Katie Lehman, you were a delightful student and now I'm learning so much from you. Karen Shuford, I so admire your teaching—please don't write a competing book. Wendy Chen Gunther, I'm hiring you to ghostwrite my next book.

To my students, both elementary- and college-age, who have given me so much joy: I'm thankful for each of you, especially those who wrote to me to say, "Help! I've just been hired as an elementary music teacher. What do I do?!" Now I can just tell you to buy my book.

Ethan, Luke, and Abigail: We lived through a pandemic as I wrote this book. I love you and am proud of you. Lois, you celebrated with me and gave me time away to write. I'm lucky to be yours.

About the Companion Website

www.oup.com/us/YourFirstYearElementaryMusic

Oxford has created a website to accompany *Your First Year as an Elementary Music Teacher: A Practical Guide for New Educators*. Material that cannot be made available in a book, namely lesson plans and printable visuals, is provided here. The reader is encouraged to consult this resource in conjunction with the chapters. Examples available online are indicated in the text with Oxford's symbol ▶.

PART I

Before Classes Begin and the First Three Weeks

Chapter 1: Start Well
Chapter 2: Meet Your Team
Chapter 3: Organize Your Room
Chapter 4: Create a Welcoming and Well-Managed Space
Chapter 5: Prepare Your Lessons

1

Start Well

Who This Book Is For

You've landed a job—congratulations! This book is written for you as you start your first year teaching elementary school music. I hope it will be a resource to you starting right now and throughout this first year teaching elementary music. With some preparation and with support from others in your building, you will have set yourself up for a successful first year in which students delight in music and you leave your workday happy.

If you just finished your music education degree and you're now starting your first job, you can do this!

If you studied music but didn't study music education, this book may be a big help to you. You haven't had the courses that will prepare your pedagogy, but you have developed your musical skills—that is important. Read this book and use it now, but plan to get additional, in-person training immediately following this year (see Chapter 11, "Become a Better Teacher"). It's not too early to start getting to know other music teachers near you and to find people who can support you.

If you don't have musical training, this book may not be what you're looking for. There certainly will be some helpful parts, but this book assumes a music background (at least an undergraduate degree) and music literacy.

If you have been teaching secondary music (band, choir, orchestra, etc.) for a while, but now are moving into an elementary music position, this book is for you, too! You already have some experience and you may choose to do some things differently than I suggest—that is absolutely fine. I hope you will find lots of direction to help ease your transition to this new context.

Just like preparing for your senior recital, excellent practice will help you to be an effective teacher. You will plan for each class and practice your plan. Then, you will perform it for students and use your improvisation skills to make it work out when it goes differently than you planned.

Your First Year as an Elementary Music Teacher. Andrew S. Paney, Oxford University Press. © Oxford University Press 2025.
DOI: 10.1093/oso/9780197631430.003.0001

You have an awesome job and will have quite a bit of choice in how your program works. As Spiderman's uncle said, "With great power comes great responsibility." You can make this first year a spectacular and memorable one.

Are you prepared for this year? No. You can't be fully prepared because you don't know what you need to know. But that's ok—no one is expecting you to know everything.

Instead, focus on preparing for each day and committing to giving your best, even if it's not exactly what you wish it was. We musicians are often critical of ourselves. Your students need *you*, not the perfect teacher. Be present for them and do your best and you will have a good year that your students will love.

Where I'm Coming From

I taught elementary students in the Chicago suburbs, in urban Fort Worth, and in the small city of Oxford, Mississippi. Now I teach teachers-in-training. I believe that children are capable of so much and that they can appreciate and make beautiful music. I believe that learning how to read and write music is essential for giving my young students the tools to make music a significant, healing part of their lives. Please note that not all music educators see the profession as I do. There are certainly other valid perspectives that also focus on training in music. I tell you mine now for the sake of transparency and so that you can know the perspective from which this book is written.

How To Use This Book

You don't need to read this book from cover to cover. Start with Part I, the first five chapters, now. Complete the checklists in these chapters as soon as possible, even before the school year starts. These chapters include some ways you can make your first teaching weeks as successful as possible. I've laid these out in the next four chapters. In Chapter 2, you'll ask, "Who do I need to know?" Since you can't know everything about the school and how to get particular supplies or tasks completed, when you know the staff at your school, you'll be happier and more prepared. But this chapter will help you prioritize your time and to meet people who will help you to immediately get your feet on the ground.

You are probably wondering how you will manage so many small children at once all by yourself. Don't worry—you can do it! Chapter 3 focuses on steps you will take to make your classroom welcoming to all children and to create a warm, kind atmosphere in which students are free to learn. This involves setting a tone for your room, determining your expectations, and thinking about how to communicate them to your students.

What do you do with your classroom? How do you prepare it for students? What if you don't have a classroom? These are questions addressed in Chapter 4. You will create a room that children enjoy visiting and that stimulates learning.

Chapter 5 is about *what* you will teach and *how*. Prior to this chapter, you will have focused on practical tasks to keep things working. This chapter is about your skills and developing those skills to help young students learn. Teachers know that there is a large difference between writing a lesson and teaching that lesson. Newer teachers benefit from practicing the *teaching* of a lesson before learning how to plan and write lessons. In this chapter, you will learn how to study and practice a lesson so that you can present it to your students in a way that will help them learn. This chapter goes hand-in-hand with Part IV of the book, the complete lessons for early elementary, intermediate, and upper elementary students.

These first five chapters are the most important for you right now. When you have read them and completed all the tasks in the checklists at the end of each chapter, you will be well prepared for your first few weeks.

Part II of the book presents issues that will arise once you're settled in with your students. Don't read it yet—focus on the first five chapters and the lessons for now. The second part of the book gives information on improving your teaching and finishing the first year well.

Part III contains games and activities you can use whenever you feel they are appropriate. Each of them has been tested with children and is written clearly so you will be successful using them.

Part IV has lessons to teach in the first three weeks, assuming you meet with students once per week. I have combined levels as much as is practically possible to help teachers have fewer lessons to study and to be able to focus on making these four preparation times extra smooth (preparing three lessons takes much less time than preparing six).

All of the activities and lessons presented in this book have been vetted by experienced teachers. Each lesson aims to hit the goals mentioned above. I expect that *you* will be able to teach these lessons and have an excellent start to the school year.

Checklists to Help You Start Well

Each chapter ends with checklists that will help you implement the suggestions in the chapter. I recommend just starting at the top of the list and doing each item in order. If there is a task that you don't need to do for your particular situation, that's perfectly fine! Just cross it off and move to the next one. You may even want to start by reading the checklists and then refer back to the chapter if something doesn't make sense to you or if you need help getting started.

Don't Be Discouraged

There will be difficulties this first year. You will probably feel underprepared and overwhelmed. Don't give up! And don't keep it to yourself. Start planning now to have a sounding board for difficult things this year. Who will it be? A family member? A good friend? A mentor?

Be resilient. Some things *are* too difficult for you, but you're *not* alone. Lean into your team and nothing can stop you. You can do this!

2

Meet Your Team

Introduction

You need people and they need you. Getting to know the people in your building will make a big difference in your success as a teacher because you will enjoy work more, get more work done, and contribute to others' success. All of this will work toward improving the health of your workplace and making your job one you will look forward to as each weekend comes to a close.

Teaching Is a Team Sport

You will get more work done when you are supported by people. Investing in people at your work helps them know you, who you are, and what you care about. When they begin to care about the things you care about, your program will experience success. Asking teachers about their families is one way to do this. Asking older teachers about what they plan to do in retirement is another way. Asking younger teachers about what kinds of things they like to watch on TV or do in town or what restaurants they enjoy eating at will help build that connection, too.

Music people need to make a special effort to be involved in the school community. It is easy to become isolated and to feel alone. You do work that is different from other teachers in your building. In addition to that, you may be coming out of a university music department that was isolated from the rest of the campus community. If you took classes in the education department of your school, you may have noticed that education majors have a different college experience than music education majors. Now is the time to reach past those differences and make connections.

You will have difficult circumstances this year. You will have situations where you don't know what to do. You will have recurring problems that you don't know how to solve. Be encouraged! No situation is irredeemable. Reflect on what's not working and

Your First Year as an Elementary Music Teacher. Andrew S. Paney, Oxford University Press. © Oxford University Press 2025.
DOI: 10.1093/oso/9780197631430.003.0002

ASK FOR HELP. The people you've already put time into knowing are the people to go to when (not if) these situations occur.

For me, the issue was classroom management. I felt like I wasn't getting to teach the things I planned to teach because just a few students were thwarting my teaching plans. I asked other teachers and even my principal for help. I told them specifically what my frustration was, what I had tried, and the result. My principal took an interest in me and recommended a small book for understanding my students better. It meant a lot to me and the act of asking for help gave us a stronger connection and investment in each other. My principal became a part of my team and I knew she was committed to my success.

Your Principal

The principal is your boss. They will make many decisions that will affect your work and your outcomes with students, so you want your principal to value what you do in your classroom and your vision for growing your program. What your principal wants is for the school to run well, for students to learn, and for teachers to be happy. How can your work support those goals? Will your students go home and tell parents how great music class is? Will parents delight in the programs you present? Will teachers at your school enjoy hearing their students sing in the halls and notice them humming songs while they're working? Can your principal stand up at the end of your program and proudly thank students and parents for their work?

Principals are busy people. How do you get to know busy people without annoying them? First, remember that they have a vested interest in your success. They hired you, or at least were involved in the hiring process, and they believe you can do this job. Not only that, but they want you to be successful. Even if they don't particularly like you, it is much easier on them to keep you for several years than to do the hiring process again. You also can make them look good and contribute to the school's culture and reputation. So, they want to know you and to take care of you. If it has been a while since you were hired, you should make it a point to visit briefly with your principal. If you see them in the hall, just walk up and say, "Hello, Ms. Brown, I'm Andy Paney, the new music teacher. So nice to see you again!" If she responds well, you have a nice little moment. If not, just say, "well, I'd better get back to it!" And excuse yourself. Even if you feel like your principal was annoyed with you, she will remember who you are and may even admire your initiative. Smile and say hello each time you see them, even casually or when they're busy.

Give your principal a personal invitation to every performance you give, whether it is in the building or on a field trip. Send them a physical note and mention it in passing in the hall or even drop in to their office to mention it. An email is appropriate, but not sufficient. In addition to your email, offer a personal visit or a paper invitation. You should expect that your principal will not be able to attend everything, but they should know what you're doing and have the chance to come to any and every performance.

One experienced teacher I spoke to as I wrote this book suggested reserving a seat for your principal at every concert, wherever they wanted to sit (front, middle, or back of the room).

My principals have generally been very supportive. If you have a principal who does not come to any performances, don't take it personally. Principals have a lot to do! Consider giving your principal a special, particular role in your program. Ask your principal to give a greeting at the beginning or end (or both!) of your program. Even better, give your principal a script to read that narrates your program or, if your principal is a musician, invite them to play or sing on some part of your program. The more specific you can make your request, the better. Consider these two requests: "I know you're a recorder player. Can you please play recorder on this piece for our concert on January 22?" and "Can you play something on our program sometime?" Which would be easier for someone to answer? Certainly the first one! Even if your principal turns down your request, you will have shown an interest in them and they will be much more likely to come to your program and to support what you're doing. At the very least, it shows your principal that you are thinking about them and planning far in advance of your program.

Office Staff

Almost everything you will need to get done will go through the front office. You want advocates and friends there who will look out for you even when you're not in the room. The workers there know what is happening in the school and can help you respond appropriately. Some things that may affect you that happen in the front office are the distribution of office supplies, purchasing, registration, scheduling, and discipline.

If you have a problem in your class with behavior, you will probably work with office staff to solve it. This might happen when a student is particularly disruptive and you seek outside help.

Office supplies (pens, paper, erasers, markers, staplers, hole punches, and more) are usually secured through the main office. When you know which things you need, make a list and take it to the office. Though they may not be able to give you everything on your list, the office staff will quickly direct you to the items you can get immediately and may direct you to how to purchase items that aren't in stock at your school.

When you purchase items for your class, you will work with office staff to find out all the steps you must take. The staff can help you with finding approved vendors (you usually can't buy from just anywhere), creating purchase orders, getting approval from appropriate administrators, and what to do when your items arrive. These tasks vary from school to school, and you will want to have help doing them correctly.

When I spent money for buying instruments or field trips, I always worked with Ms. Rivera. Ms. Rivera was a quiet lady, but she regularly showed her exasperation with me, especially with regard to my mistakes in the forms for spending money. I read everything carefully and made sure I was following protocol, but I made mistakes or misunderstood timing or other issues. Ms. Rivera would sigh and show me (without words) her frustration. I had to work with her regularly and I always tried to be kind and positive, but she continued to be unhappy with me. Eventually I said to her, "I'm sorry about the mistakes I'm making. I'm working hard to do this right and I want you to know that I'm not doing this to annoy you!" I thought it was a risky thing to say, but it actually did make a difference. We had a much more cordial relationship after that. I wonder sometimes if she just wanted me to be aware of the extra work I was causing her.

I've found that office staff are perhaps the main advocates for my program and my students when I am not in the room. Office staff tend to have very good memories and remember the things I've requested in the past and the values I have for my program. This means that when another teacher or even the principal suggests something that may be difficult for me, for instance, having my choir perform at a meeting before school on a Monday, that the office staff will speak up and tell them that that probably won't work for our group and that we need more preparation time or that we only perform during the school day.

Custodial Staff

Many custodial staff are ignored by both teachers and students. Seek out those who clean and service your building. Learn their names and what they like. Bring them small gifts when you have a chance, like a $5 coffee gift card or a greeting card acknowledging their work on your behalf. This is particularly important after a program. Your program will probably involve extra cleaning for the custodial staff. It may also involve quite a bit of time setting up chairs and preparing a space. A thank you note can go a long way to build your team!

Here are some things that custodial staff generally do that will affect you daily: cleaning the classrooms, emptying garbage, vacuuming the floors, clearing and cleaning marker boards, rearranging seats and desks, and locking classrooms at the end of the day. When you have a program, they will do additional work, including cleaning the performance space before the event, setting up chairs and other furniture, moving instruments (sometimes including the piano), setting up audiovisual equipment, working lights and climate control for the performance space, and clearing and cleaning the performance space after the program.

How do you get custodial help? The first step is to ask the office staff, "I need _______ for my program next week. Is there a particular process to request the help of custodial staff?" You will then find out if you need any special approvals or if you need to fill out a form. The office staff may just tell you to ask the custodial staff. Either way, it would be good to touch base with the custodial staff to let them know what you need and when and whether you've filled out the necessary paperwork. The earlier you can do this, the better.

You can ask for the office to contact custodial staff for your projects. But it is often better to ask the custodial staff yourself. Then you can ask in a kind way and build that relationship rather than having the order come down from the top (the main office or the principal). If you do ask directly, let the office know what you have requested so that they know that the custodial staff have more tasks than usual and that other less urgent tasks may take a back burner.

Other Teachers

Be proactive in making a wonderful workspace: bring food, volunteer, be positive in your speech (no complaining), go to happy hours, and go to celebrations. Other teachers at an elementary school generally spend a lot of time with a few students. You, as the music teacher, will see lots of students for much less time each week. Classroom teachers are an invaluable part of your success with students. Classroom teachers can help you avoid problems with behavior and with managing overly involved parents. They can support your goals and help with making your program a success.

My sister-in-law, Amy, is a special education teacher at a small school in Michigan. She brought some home-baked goods to school one day and left them in the teachers' lounge. She noticed how appreciative teachers were and started to bring baked treats every Monday of the year. She would seek out recipes and vary her offering each week. She enjoyed making things and the other teachers looked forward to Mondays. This was a way she contributed to a positive work environment. During COVID-19 restrictions, she switched to individually packaged goods, but still with a theme of some sort. I loved this idea because it was something she took joy in thinking about and doing and it made a difference for the people she worked with.

Avoid complaining or talking about students. When you see other teachers over lunch or in a planning period it is tempting to vent, especially if you have a particularly challenging student. Do vent! But don't talk about particular students in your venting. Do ask teachers for advice dealing with a difficult student, but don't do this in the context of a vent.

I found that older teachers in my school were much more likely to talk about travel, food, gardening, events, and books than about students. I found this a refreshing, adult break from the world of working with kids. I felt rejuvenated and ready for the rest of my day.

You should know the names of all the teachers in your building, but take a particular effort to know the teachers who have classrooms close to yours. They may be affected by the sounds coming from your classroom and you will want them to be understanding! You may also be able to work with them to address behavior problems (see Chapter 4)

Parents

Parents are an important part of your long-term success. Successful music programs have parent support and those with strong support are much more stable and less at risk for budget (or other) cuts. You probably don't need to know every parent in the school, but you do need to be kind and remember that they are important.

Times when you are likely to meet parents are on the first day of school, before or after school, at an open house, or at your concert. Remember, they love their children and see them through eyes of love. Always talk about their child with care and kindness. For that matter, always talk about every child with care and kindness.

In my first year of teaching, I mainly talked to parents when I called them to talk about their child's behavior in my class. Though I worked hard to speak professionally, it would have been better if I were contacting to tell them something positive as my first contact. Does a child complete an assignment or task with excellence? Call their home and let their caretakers know! Send home a hand-written note, if that's possible. Or even email them! It doesn't need to be long or perfectly written, just a quick, "Dear _____, I wanted you to know what a nice job _______ did with our instrument assignment today. The class enjoyed his creation and I hope you will celebrate him, too! Sincerely, Andy Paney." These little gestures often make a lasting impact. The parents are likely to remember what you said and to think positively of your program and of you as a teacher. They are also more likely to mention you to the principal and to other parents.

Invite parents to help you. Do you need help with setup for a program? Ask a parent if they can come early to help. These requests always work better when asked directly to one person, rather than a general appeal for help. If you have a good connection with a parent (perhaps because you've contacted them about their child's good work) ask them if they'd be able to help you for a particular task. It's probably best to make the request very clear and with a defined end: "I was wondering if you could help me with setup for our program next month. I would need you to show up two hours before the performance to help with decorations. I'll ask someone else to help with clean up afterward. Would that work for you?" This allows them to know what they are committing to and know that they won't be there forever (or have to help you every time). This is in contrast to, "Can you please help out with the music sometimes?"—a much more open-ended request that doesn't let them know the scope of the task you're asking them to do.

Acknowledge the role of parents at programs. Thank them. Acknowledge particular parents who have helped out: "I'm thankful for each of you parents, grandparents, and guardians. You have worked with your children outside of school time to help them get ready for this. I'm especially thankful for Mr. Garcia, Ms. Smith, and Mr. Nguyen and their work getting this room looking so good for our program. Can we please get a round of applause for them?" A nice, handwritten note (short) is a good gesture for these people, too.

Your Community

Knowing the community in which you teach will affect your choices of repertoire and how you teach. Students' learning occurs within the context of their culture. If you live in the community where you teach, great! If not, plan to drive around the places that feed into your school. Consider getting lunch or dinner in that area and bumping into students and their caregivers. Ask people for specific help that you think they would gladly give. This will be a long-term process, but make a plan for it. Teachers who know the contexts of their students teach them better.[1]

Outside Support

You can find groups of music teachers on most social media platforms. These places are great for new teachers because of the quick, wise responses you can get to questions you ask. Experienced teachers are often delighted to support someone new to the profession. You will be welcomed into a community that knows what you're experiencing and is rooting for your success.

Keep in touch with your family, friends, and former teachers, too. These aren't people you need to meet, but I include them here because you will benefit from keeping them in the loop about how things are going in your work. Tell them explicitly that you are starting a new, difficult job, and that you want their support, especially in this first year. Be sure to tell them what things are going well and where the difficulties are. Keep regular phone or text or email conversations going with just one or two people. Check in and tell them how each week is going.

Checklist for Meeting Your Team

- ☐ Introduce yourself to one person in the office.
- ☐ Introduce yourself to one person on the custodial staff.
- ☐ Introduce yourself to your principal (or one of your principals).
- ☐ Introduce yourself to one teacher who has a room close to your space.
- ☐ Later: Find three people to be your partners this year: a teacher you see often, another music teacher at the same career stage, and a more experienced music teacher.

3

Organize Your Room

Introduction

By the end of this chapter, your classroom will be a place that delights children and that they eagerly anticipate visiting each week. Your room will stimulate their curiosity, discourage distraction, and help guide them to making music without unnecessary temptations. We'll work through four areas to get your room ready for the school year:

Clear the junk.
Create seating charts.
Make a plan for students' entry and exit.
Display stimulating visuals throughout the room.

Clear the Junk

If you don't have a classroom, skip down to the "If You Don't Have A Classroom" section at the end of this chapter.

First things first: there's so much stuff! You will probably find your music room packed full of books, instruments, and more. In my experience, music rooms tend to gather new things and almost never get cleared out.

Do not throw books or instruments away, no matter how bad their condition. Your school has a procedure for disposing of them. Just gather them together, take photos of them, and place them neatly somewhere where they will not disturb your teaching. Eventually, you'll want to list the items that need to be replaced, suggest appropriate and up-to-date replacements, and make a request of your principal or your parent-teacher association or organization (PTA or PTO). Include the list and photos in your request to build your case that they need to be replaced.

Your First Year as an Elementary Music Teacher. Andrew S. Paney, Oxford University Press. © Oxford University Press 2025.
DOI: 10.1093/oso/9780197631430.003.0003

Do not be surprised if your room has several music textbooks series dating back to the 1950s (or before). It's easy to think, "These could come in handy sometime!" and if you have space in your room to organize them and use them, fine! If not, stack them up and plan to replace them or just dispose of them later.

If your room is home to many instruments—great! That will be good for you and for your students. Students will be tempted to play any instruments they see. Find a place for your instruments that keeps them out of reach of students in their assigned seats and that gives you space for your instruction. Instruments don't all have to be accessible all the time. Shelves and closets can help organize, protect, and preserve them for when you need them. Again, instruments that are no longer useful should be photographed and stored where they won't interfere with your work or students' learning.

Visual Aids and Posters

Quickly sort through any posters and other visual aids you find. Later in this chapter you'll start decorating your room, so put aside anything you particularly like. Don't plan to sort everything into perfect categories—you can do that later. Instead, sort into just two stacks: things you like and things you don't like. It's usually ok to throw out posters or other items that won't be listed on the school's inventory of purchases.

The Piano

It can be difficult to choose a place for the piano, especially if it's a grand or a tall upright. If you plan to use the piano with students, look for a place that will allow you to see all of your students while at the piano. Avoid having your back to your students. Using the piano with students is certainly not required, but it is nice to have some live, harmonic accompaniment on occasion. If you don't plan to play the piano in your lessons, place it so students can see the keys. This can be a helpful visual aid, especially when you teach half steps and whole steps or key signatures.

Everyday Items

Items you will use every day deserve their own special place: dry erase markers, erasers, pens, pencils, seating charts, recordings, your computer, tuning fork, and more. The marker board or chalkboard in your room can be a huge help for these things. Buy some strong magnets and glue them to little baskets or containers to have a place to store each of these things on your board. You can also glue or tape the magnets directly to the items. Having a place where you always keep these things will make your life easier! You will regularly want to reach for one of these items and having it always in the same, accessible place will make a big difference to you and to your students.

You will need a way to share musical recordings with your students. If you have a device in your room, decide on a place to put it where you can access it easily and quickly while teaching. Also, be sure the speakers fill the room with sound. Students should experience music, especially music that is new to them, with the highest sound quality you can provide. Do not use your phone's speaker—that is made for you alone (or maybe with one friend) to listen to. Your students will not get an accurate perception of the music you play for them without appropriately sized speakers.

Where Will the Students Be?

Seating in a music classroom can be a challenge because you may have children as young as 4 and as old as 12 learning in the same space. Set up your room to have flexibility for different ages and types of activities.

Sitting on the Floor

Your younger students, ages 4–7, will do just fine sitting on the floor, but don't expect larger children (age 9 and up) to sit on the floor for the full lesson. When younger students sit on the floor, even just for one activity, plan for where each child will be—what is their spot? If you have a large rug in your class, you can just say, "Put your toes on the edge of the rug." If you don't, find a way to mark where students should be. You can use painter's tape to put an X where each student should sit or stand. If your room has a noncarpeted floor, use a permanent marker to make a small mark directly on the floor.[1]

Sitting on Chairs

Chairs help with discipline, taking roll, and singing posture. They give students their own space and can help with discipline problems that arise from having everyone close together on the floor with less defined spaces. They will also help you with knowing who is absent—it's easy to notice an empty chair. Children who have difficulties with mobility often do better with chairs, too, and students in wheelchairs or other assistive devices will more likely be at the same level as other students (rather than having their heads a few feet above their peers who are sitting on the floor).[2] Sitting on chairs can also encourage singing posture.

Plan to have children sit in chairs and to use chairs in your room and create a large area on the floor for movement activities and for instruments. Here are some tips for arranging the classroom:

1. Find out the number of students in your largest class. Ask at the office or ask another teacher what the cap is for classes at your school.
2. Organize your room to fit your largest class.
3. Aim for two rows of chairs or at most three. It's better to not have students in many rows. In a smaller room, an L-shape will often accommodate an entire class and still give room for movement activities.

Create Seating Charts

A seating chart will help you with discipline, with learning students' names, and with using time efficiently. There is no better way to learn students' names, and you won't have to solve the problem of students arguing with each other about where they sit. Students are accustomed to seating charts and feel comfortable having their own space.

Instead of using a digital seating chart on a tablet or phone, I recommend using a paper seating chart so that you can ensure it is always visible to you without having to change apps or unlock a screen. Some tips for making seating charts:

Have a single page for each class. It might help to have a separate clipboard for each day and have that day's seating charts clipped together in the order you will see the classes.

Your seating chart can have areas for assessment, too. Make little boxes on each and specify what will go in each box. Then you will have a record of progress for your students (Figure 3.1).

You need a list of students to make your seating charts. Ask at the office for the class lists for all the teachers in your school. This is where those relationships will come in

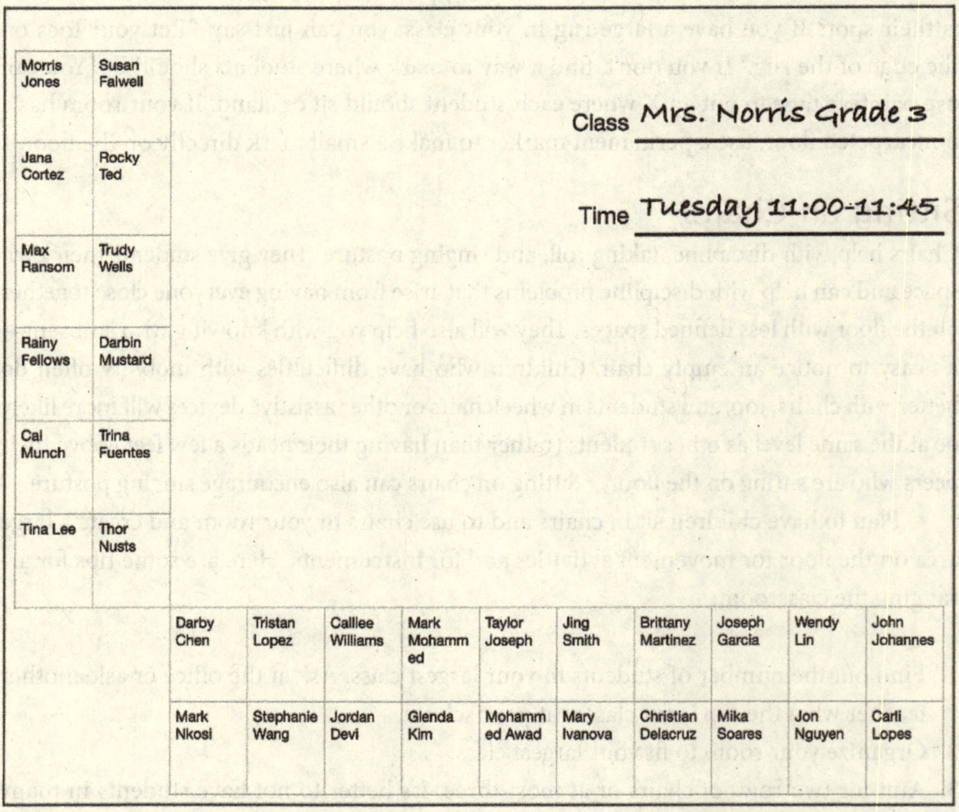

Class Mrs. Norris Grade 3

Time Tuesday 11:00-11:45

Morris Jones	Susan Falwell
Jana Cortez	Rocky Ted
Max Ransom	Trudy Wells
Rainy Fellows	Darbin Mustard
Cal Munch	Trina Fuentes
Tina Lee	Thor Nusts

Darby Chen	Tristan Lopez	Caillee Williams	Mark Mohammed	Taylor Joseph	Jing Smith	Brittany Martinez	Joseph Garcia	Wendy Lin	John Johannes
Mark Nkosi	Stephanie Wang	Jordan Devi	Glenda Kim	Mohammed Awad	Mary Ivanova	Christian Delacruz	Mika Soares	Jon Nguyen	Carli Lopes

FIGURE 3.1 An example of a seating chart. See the online supplement for a blank one you can use.

handy (see Chapter 2)! Expect there to be changes to your rosters when the year begins (and throughout the year).

Make a Plan for Students' Entry and Exit

It's likely that classes of students will be coming to you one right after the other with no passing period or transition time. Often music teachers have one class that ends at, say, 9:40 and another that begins at 9:40. How do you manage that transition?

Having clear procedures for beginning class and ending class will benefit both you and your students. If you have two doors to your classroom, consider having an "In" door and an "Out" door. You can have students line up at the "Out" door at 9:39 and do some activities with them in line while they wait for their teacher to arrive (see Chapter 12 for activities to do while students are waiting in line). If the second class arrives before the first leaves, you can have them go right to their assigned seats, since they've already been vacated. You can even do some activities with both classes, if necessary. You also have helped avoid having students bump into each other "by accident" and talk to each other because they're close by. If you only have one door, you can make it work with some creativity. You might have the departing class line up against one wall, giving lots of space to the arriving class.

You will also need to help other teachers get on board with your plan. Make large, clear signs that will make it easy for teachers to know exactly what to do and where to go. You want the classroom teachers to have a positive first music experience, too! Remind them when they drop off the students what will happen when they come back to pick them up.

Display Stimulating Visuals Throughout the Room

Your room can stimulate your students' minds and can pique their interest in things they haven't yet experienced, like music from a different culture. Give thought to the items in your room and what you hang on your walls; consider how you can capture the curiosity of students whose minds wander. Plan for your room to support concepts you teach, enrich students' minds, and invite your students to know who you are.

I can't stress enough the value of having a wide range of visuals in your room. The music that you know and love may be a complete mystery to many students in your school. It's possible they will never have heard classical music or jazz or even pop music. Children have different backgrounds and most likely listen to what their parents like—not necessarily what is popular in your area. This is a great opportunity to teach students the extremely broad range of music that exists in the world! Start with planning to have visual representations of music from at least two different traditions in the world (e.g., a symphony orchestra and a Chinese opera or a Bluegrass band and a gamelan). Add to your classroom as you get to know your community. Do you have a large Filipino community? Find some photos to display (and plan to use some music in your lessons, too). Your neighbors may have some items (and songs) they'd love to share! You want your students to see themselves *and* others in the music in your room.

Your room will be a place where students learn, but it should also be a place you enjoy spending most of your day. Make your room *your* place: a place that reflects what you care about. This means having a place for your personal items and displaying some things that give your students a taste of what you enjoy doing and talking about.

To start, I recommend adding one item from each of the three categories below. Then plan to add to your room every week or two.

Add Some Color

- A map of the world.
- Instruments and their families from various cultures.
- Composers' portraits and biographies: consider making your own or making some with a music teacher friend, printing multiple copies, and sharing them. Sets that you can purchase are almost all of long-dead, white men. Include some great women and composers of color, old and new.

Stimulate Understanding

- Solfège syllables.
- Musical terms: pianissimo, piano, mezzo piano, mezzo forte, forte, fortissimo, etc.
- Music notes.
- Voice biology.
- Lists of music you will listen to.
- Common forms with example songs (for example, "Twinkle Twinkle Little Star" is ABA or "London Bridge" is strophic).
- Lyrics to songs you're teaching.
- A code wall: songs in only rhythm notation that students will decipher and name. You can put students' names on the board when they figure one out. Consider adding a new one each week without removing the older ones.

Share Who You Are

- Include photos of yourself doing things you love to do.
- Add posters from your favorite musicals, operas, oratorios, bands, traditional musics, etc.
- Use colors and items that *you* like.

If You Don't Have a Classroom

If you don't have a classroom, you have different problems to address. A priority for you is to get seating charts. Ask teachers for copies of their seating charts at the beginning of the year and be prepared to edit them regularly. Teachers may invite you to use their seating charts while you're in their room. This offer, though kind, will probably not help you to learn students' names and to keep track of student learning. Instead, make a copy that you can write on and take with you. See "Creating Seating Charts" section above for some ways you can use them to make your life easier.

You can't decorate other people's classrooms, but you will still benefit from using visual aids and by making each classroom yours. There are two ways to do this: bring visual aids with you and use digital visual aids.

Using digital visual aids is a good way to have a visually stimulating lesson and to be able to show your students musical examples. One problem is that you can't count on technology to always work correctly, especially if you are moving from room to room and having to connect and disconnect from others' projectors or computers. I don't recommend relying on connecting your own computer to a different projector or trying to open your own files from a portable drive on someone else's computer. There are too many possibilities for error and, even if it works, you can't count on it being a quick setup. Instead, if the internet is reliable in your building, use a cloud service like Google Docs and set the permissions to open for anyone with the link. Then you can place your visual aids in an online folder that will sync automatically and be the same on any computer, regardless of age or brand (as long as it connects to the internet). I use a web shortener that allows custom links to make it easy for me to access my visual aids. Then, when I present, I type into the computer the easy, short address (e.g., http://tiny.cc/andysfolder) and have immediate access. If this is not an option, I recommend creating folders on your computer for each grade level (not each class). Then you can easily find the material you need for each class.

Even if you have dependable internet in your building, sometimes chart paper is the best, most reliable way to present your visual aids. Here are some ideas for visual aids that could travel with you to each classroom you visit:

- Chart paper (24 by 32 inches or larger) and chart markers (buy at an office supply store or order online, if you can't get them quickly through your school—they're not expensive).
- Smaller visual aids, about the size of a piece of paper, with magnets you can use on the board in another teacher's room.
- A portable speaker. You can use it along with your phone for listening lessons.

Checklist for Organizing Your Room

Use this list to prepare your classroom for the first day of class. Just start at the top and work your way down and you'll be ready to go!

Clear the Junk

- ☐ Decide which books you will use and which you will store.
- ☐ Sort your instruments into working/nonworking and find places to store the instruments that are not in good shape.
- ☐ Put instruments you plan to use in accessible, but not distracting, places.
- ☐ Sort visual aids and posters into two stacks: Use and Discard. Then discard one of the piles.
- ☐ Take photos of items in your room that need to be replaced or that you would like removed and place them in a digital folder.
- ☐ Choose a suitable place for the piano (don't worry, you can move it later if necessary).
- ☐ Choose a place for items you will use daily: dry erase markers, erasers, pens, pencils, seating charts, recordings, your computer, tuning fork, and more. Remember that magnets can be a big help to place things on your marker board.

Create Seating Charts—Yes or No Questions

1. Have you chosen your room setup, including where students will sit?
2. Have you considered the mobility and access needs of diverse learners in your room setup?
3. Have you designed a seating chart template that matches your room setup and fits your largest class?
4. Have you filled out your seating charts for each class that will arrive?

Make a Plan for Students' Entry and Exit—Yes or No Questions

1. Have you decided how students will enter and leave the room?
2. Have you made signs that teachers and students can easily follow?

Display Stimulating Visuals Throughout the Room—Yes or No Questions

1. Have you hung at least four items on your walls (see list above for suggestions)?
2. Does your classroom include visuals from more than one musical tradition?
3. Does your room have some color?
4. Does your room have something that is uniquely "you?"

If You Don't Have a Classroom—Yes or No Questions

1. Have you requested seating charts from all teachers in your school?
2. Have you made copies of all seating charts?
3. Do you have a plan for sharing visual and audio examples with your students?
4. Have you made some visual aids that travel well?
5. Do you have a travel speaker?

4

Create a Welcoming and Well-Managed Space

Introduction

The music class can be an oasis of beauty that children love visiting. In this chapter you will find ways to build a welcoming, inclusive, positive classroom, where children can be at their best. In addition to the magic, there must be learning! You will need to establish some routines and to let students know about your expectations of them. You will also need to remind them and let them know that you're serious about keeping the environment a positive place for all to learn. Just as you will ask students to meet expectations, you yourself will choose a positive attitude and work to proactively build an environment with clear expectations and procedures for students.

There are many excellent books and articles on creating a well-managed and happy classroom. Many of these are targeted to specific populations or contexts.[1] I recommend asking your principal or the teachers in your school what they recommend. If there is a book or approach that most teachers in your building use and buy into, it will benefit you to know it and to use it. In this chapter, I'll touch on some of the most important and most time-sensitive ways to prepare for an enjoyable first few weeks of teaching.

Create a Positive Atmosphere

I taught in an urban school in Texas and had some discipline problems that I couldn't seem to work out like students talking out of turn, refusing to do work, and interrupting me. I talked with my principal and with other music teachers in similar schools and they recommended solutions that helped tremendously. The teachers suggested I use consistently positive language and build trust with my students.[2] I started saying regularly, "I'm so glad to be here with you this morning to work on this music," "I'm excited

Your First Year as an Elementary Music Teacher. Andrew S. Paney, Oxford University Press. © Oxford University Press 2025.
DOI: 10.1093/oso/9780197631430.003.0004

to be working on this together," "It is great to see all of you again," and other positive, we're-all-in-this-together-type statements. It felt corny to me and I sometimes said it before I felt it, but I noticed a big change. The change was in my students' responses to me, but also in my feelings about my students and my attitude toward my work. Of course, these should be true statements, not empty praise but expressions of your enjoyment of them.

Increase your Pace

The pacing of your lesson will make a big difference in how your students respond. Often children's talking when they are excited can be difficult to manage. But the students may not be doing anything wrong, they're just loving music class! Keeping a quick pace will prevent this talking problem. It will also help prevent other behavior issues because students will not have a chance to formulate their plans.

In order to have a quick pace, you will have to prepare, prepare, and prepare some more. This is the only way to make smooth, quick transitions between activities. The time between when you finish one activity and begin the next should be less than one second—really! As you're finishing one thing, be thinking about the next.

If you sing two songs back to back, you will probably want to be preparing for the second song before the first song ends. You need to know the key, tempo, first pitch, and first words and be ready to introduce them as soon as the other song ends.

Make a list of some things you can do if you need a couple more seconds to transition. For instance, you might have young students pat their heads or clap (or, even better, stomp) a rhythm after you. Anything you can do to keep things moving will help you and add to students' joy.

Decide How to Prepare

What will it take for you to feel prepared for the first day of school? What do you want to have ready? Make a list—it's ok if it's long. Then work through that list one item at a time. When you reach the end, be confident that you have prepared as well as you know how. Keep in mind that you will probably miss some things and make some mistakes. Accept it. You're new, remember? I mention this because so many of us musicians have tendencies toward perfectionism. Allow yourself some room to grow this first year.

How you plan your lessons will make a huge difference. Plan for more material than you believe you will be able to cover and practice doing it. Practice saying the words aloud and going through the motions. Practice with a smile and aim for clear and precise language to communicate what students should do.

Set Your Expectations

Nothing discourages teachers more than out-of-control students. But even the toughest teaching assignments are possible with good planning and collaboration. You need a plan. What are the rules in your classroom? I suggest using these:

Show Respect.
Follow Directions.
Do Your Best.

Though the number of rules is few, students learn what each of those means. I tell them the first day what it means to "show respect." We show respect to other students by keeping our hands to ourselves, by speaking kindly, and by looking out for their interests. We show respect to teachers by raising our hand before speaking (this also respects other students), by following directions, by remaining in our seat, by participating in class activities, by listening. We show respect to tools in the classroom by caring for instruments and using them correctly, by cleaning up after ourselves, and by taking turns.

Following directions means doing what the teacher asks you to do. Though that may sound authoritarian, we hope that our directions will be inclusive and thoughtful. We want students to experience the best class period possible and we are the ones who have spent the most time planning for the period. We will follow the plan! If students want to plan a class period or a section of class period, we will all follow their directions, too. To do great things together, we need to follow the lead of someone who has put thought into how our work will go. We certainly can offer input and suggestions, but we agree, as a group, to follow the leader.

Doing your best means working hard to improve your skills. It means that you are aiming today to do better than you did yesterday. This does not mean you will be perfect or even that you should aim to be perfect. We want to challenge each other to be improving. This is particularly important for your perfectionist students. Some may be frustrated that they can't do something as well as they'd like to. Remind them regularly that they will get there, and that you want them to do their best now, even if it's not at the level they'd like it to be. This rule also applies to students who are not perfectionists and may choose to be silly or to do something other than what you have asked for. Gently remind them to do their best on the task. Tell them that you follow that rule, too: "I want you, my students, to help *me* become a better teacher. I hope you will let me help you become a better musician."

Don't Present Your Class Rules, Teach Them

Teaching your rules on the first day helps set the tone for your class. The tone should be encouraging and not discouraging. We show students that we expect them to get a lot out of the class periods they have with us and to allow others to do the same. We want to inspire them and teach them how to have the best experience in our classroom. This should be done with a smile and with optimism for how they will do. Even saying, "I know you care about growing and want to be better at music at the end of the year. Let's work together to get there!" can be powerful for students.

Modeling is a particularly effective teaching tool. Plan to model your class rules and what it looks like to follow them and not to follow them. For instance, you might say something like, "When it's time to sing together, we all will do our best. If I am sitting like this [slouch, frown, and keep your lips tightly clenched], am I doing my best singing?" "What about when I sit like this [sit up and sing a phrase of a known song like "Twinkle Twinkle Little Star"]?" Give positive and negative models of each classroom expectation.

Get Everyone on Board with Class Routines

Your classroom is a place for *all* of your students to learn. Having clear routines and expectations will be particularly important for some of your students. Students with differing abilities, especially those who are on the autism spectrum, will benefit from knowing what is going to happen. Students with mobility issues will be glad to know when they will need to move and when they won't. Routines make your room a place of comfort and safety for as many of your students as possible. See Chapter 12 for suggestions for beginning and ending class.

Some routines to consider developing for your particular teaching situation include:

How class begins.
How class ends.
How you take roll (if you are required to).
How to get instruments out.
What to do when you have an instrument.
How to put instruments away.
How to get in specific formations: circle, two lines, double circle, etc.

When There Is a Problem in the Classroom

There will be times when students do not follow your rules and create a problem for you or for other students. Don't be surprised—remind yourself that this is normal. You want to respond kindly and to give the child the benefit of the doubt, even if you feel personally attacked by the situation. Do not ignore the problem, but respond in a calm voice and remind students of your expectations. Ask the office staff if there is a school-wide way to handle discipline problems. If there is, follow it! This will make it easier for you and your students because they will know what to expect and have a standard process in all of their classes. If your school doesn't have a policy on this, you will need to create your own. Here is a possible approach:

- As soon as you see *any* action that does not fit your classroom rules, remind the whole group about the rules and what the specific rule you believe is not being followed is. Give a positive way to deal with the situation that contrasts with what you observed.
- If there is a second action, address the child or children by name, again gently, and remind them the rule and suggest a way they can do what they're doing that does meet the class rules.
- If there is a third action, continue to keep the emotional pressure low. Ask the child or children to stop what they're doing and relocate them to different part of the classroom. If more than one student was involved, be sure to move them apart from each other, preferably without direct sight lines.

With older students, it's possible that one student's disruption will lead to other students' disruptions, too. If you come down hard on one student, you may find other students sticking up for that student and the classroom increasingly getting out of your control.

Instead, be respectful and firm. Emphasize the importance of everyone learning: "My job is to teach *every* person in this class how to be a better musician. We do that by following our three rules."

Equity and Equality

Aim for equity rather than equality in your classroom. Equality means that everyone is treated equally and has the exact same opportunities and experiences in your class. Equity, on the other hand, is about being fair and impartial. Your students are not all the same. They have lived through different experiences and have different needs than you, I, or their classmates have. For this reason, plan to have some flexibility in how you address students in your classroom. Some students may require more of your time and different responses from you. If other students point out your "unfairness," just politely mention that your job is to help everyone in your classroom to grow. I like to mention in all my classes that I want each person in the room to move forward in their skills. This means that not everyone will reach the same level, but that everyone will grow.

Reset the Classroom

One routine that you will never regret implementing is training the students to reset the classroom at the end of each class period. Before each class leaves, have students help you reset the room: put the chairs back where they go, pick up any trash, clear the board, clean the board, put markers, erasers, etc., back where they go. Build this into your daily plan so that students grow to expect it and even look forward to it. You can lead this each time, or, if you prefer, you can create a checklist on a poster or on your shared computer screen. Instead of calling this "clean up time," I recommend using something like "reset time." This slight change of wording makes it a more positive activity for students and allows them to think about what has changed over the music period and what they can do to reset the room. Here are some items I'd put on the checklist:

Put chairs on their marks (or align them so you have straight lines).
Put away instruments.
Put away anything else.
Erase the marker board.
Put markers and erasers in their proper places.
Check for garbage throughout the room and put it in the trashcan.
Sit in your place until dismissed to line up.

Checklist for Creating a Welcoming Space

Use this list to help you prepare for your students and their unique personalities and needs.

Create a Positive Atmosphere

- ☐ Choose some phrases you can say to your students to show you are glad to be their teacher and are happy to be with them, for instance: "I'm so glad to be with you today," "I'm excited to work on this with you this morning," or "It makes me happy to see each of you in this class."
- ☐ Practice saying the phrases you choose aloud and imagine saying them in your classroom.

Improve Your Pace

- ☐ Practice the transitions between activities or songs until you can do them in less than one second.
- ☐ Make a list of some things you can do if you need a couple more seconds with younger students.
- ☐ Make another list for older students.

Decide How to Prepare

- ☐ Make a list of everything you would like to have done before classes begin—everything!
- ☐ Write down somewhere, in your planner or on a sticky note, "It's ok to make mistakes. I'll get better at this!"

Set Your Expectations

☐ Decide on 3–5 rules you want to use in your classroom. Mine are: Show Respect, Follow Directions, and Do Your Best.

☐ Make a poster of your classroom rules or use the model in ▶Visual 15.2.

Teach Your Expectations

☐ Make a plan for how you will teach your rules in class.

☐ Add to your plan specific examples of how students can follow the rules and break the rules in classroom situations: using instruments, taking turns, answering or asking a question, speaking to other students, or cleaning after themselves.

Get Everyone on Board with Class Routines

☐ Write out specific steps for students to take when they do the following activities. This is for your eyes only.

- How class begins (See Chapter 12 for some ideas).
- How class ends (See Chapter 12 for some ideas).
- How you take roll (if you are required to).
- How to get instruments out.
- What to do when you have an instrument.
- How to put instruments away.
- How to get in specific formations: circle, two lines, double circle, etc.

When There Is a Problem in the Classroom

☐ Decide how you will respond when a child breaks one of your rules. Plan to not let things slide, but address them gently, firmly, and with kindness.

Reset the Classroom

☐ Decide on the items you'd like to have set before each class.

☐ Write those items down for yourself and, perhaps, for your students, too.

☐ Plan to teach the reset on the first day of class and repeat it on the second.

☐ Work this into your daily routine and don't miss it!

5

Prepare Your Lessons

Introduction

Conductors prepare for a performance by studying the score and planning rehearsals. They know the score extremely well and are able to help performers reach their expectations for the work. For elementary music teachers, a lot of the same requirements apply. We must know each of our songs or rhymes extremely well. We must plan how we will present and teach them to young students. This chapter introduces the rest of the book and gives context for how to prepare the first lessons you will teach.

What to Include in an Elementary Music Class

Musical Skills

The National Core Arts Standards (NCAS, https://www.nationalartsstandards.org/) describe the teaching and learning that should happen in any music classroom. All learning falls under one of these headings: Creating, Performing/Producing/Presenting, Responding, and Connecting. Based on those standards, here is a list of musical skills I use in my teaching of music.

- Listen.
- Audiate.
- Memorize.
- Read.
- Write.
- Create [improvise and compose].
- Sing.
- Play [instruments].
- Move [conduct and dance].

Your First Year as an Elementary Music Teacher. Andrew S. Paney, Oxford University Press. © Oxford University Press 2025.
DOI: 10.1093/oso/9780197631430.003.0005

• Synthesize.
• Contextualize.[1]

No person has fully mastered any one of these skills—even professional musicians can grow in each of these areas. In each class, we work to help each student move forward on each of those skills. As they grow, they can use these skills for creating music and performing in ways that highlight their creativity, and aren't limited to our strengths as teachers. These skills align with the NCAS artistic processes of Creating (write, create), Performing/Producing/Presenting (sing, play, move), Responding (listen, audiate, memorize, read), and Connecting (synthesize and contextualize).[2] Of course, all of these skills can fit into more than one category. We'll discuss more in Chapter 6.

Your students will develop these skills through the activities you plan and do with them: songs and rhymes, instrument lessons, music activities, and listening lessons.

Most of your lesson sections will includes songs and rhymes. This is the easiest way to get students doing music. One difficulty for us music teachers is learning the songs well enough to teach them.

You will teach instrumental skills in your class this year, too. As with any music lesson, this will require careful planning for your students to be successful.

I use "music activities" as a catch-all for other things that might occur during music lessons: games, preparing for performances, worksheets, and other creative items that don't fit into the above categories.

You may think that a listening activity will be a break for you or will be good if you run out of time. Unfortunately, listening lessons won't save you. These lessons are so hard to teach. You will spend as much more time preparing a listening lesson as any other type of lesson.

When you have students listen to music, be sure you are using a medium or larger speaker. Small speakers, like those built into your phone or tablet, are difficult to hear in a large room with dozens of people. Allow students the pleasure of hearing all music in high quality without distortion.

Deliver Lessons so Students Learn

This may be the simplest and perhaps the most often overlooked truism: If your students aren't learning, you're not teaching. Teaching requires learning. This is not about guilt or about labeling people "bad" (or "good") teachers. This is about getting a perspective on learning how to be better at reaching students. You can't find the one right way to teach and just keep doing it. You must connect with *those* students, the ones in *your* class. Just because you have had success in the past doesn't mean that you can keep doing the same thing. You will figure out what the students in the room need and you will do it.

For me this was a humbling lesson. I was teaching middle school choir at an urban middle school and I was really excited about it. I had chosen great music to teach and sing and had prepared really fun activities to help with learning rhythms and pitches. I knew my students would really enjoy my class. But they didn't follow me. They didn't do what I asked. Activities that I knew would be fun were not fun because they didn't trust me. Or maybe they were just "bad kids." But they *should* be able to do this! I *shouldn't* have to adjust my lesson. They needed to learn to get on board. Fortunately, other teachers helped me address this problem. Based on their advice, I tried being positive in my attitude and in my language (see Chapter 4). I changed my approach and had better results.

Should I have had to do that? Probably not. Should students just be well-behaved? Probably so. But, as one of my mentors taught me, we don't live in the land of "should."[3] We take students as they are and hope to move them closer to what they can be. Their learning is more important to me than my desire to get what I deserve or that I can teach the way I want to teach.

How do you teach so that students learn? Here are some thoughts:

I. **Look at your students.** You will know if they're learning if you're actively involved in watching them. A rookie teaching mistake is to be self-focused: Am I presenting this correctly? Am I remembering my plan? What do I say next? Good teachers are looking at their students and tracking how they are doing. Do they understand? Are they on the same page? You will be able to teach when you are regularly assessing and not saving assessment for an exam.

II. **Model what you want.** If you want them to sing, you need to sing. If you want them to sing in tune, you need to sing in tune for them every time you sing. Model the correct way and the incorrect way. Just saying, "I don't want that note to be flat," is not nearly as powerful as singing the phrase with the note flat, then immediately singing it with it in tune.

III. **Be positive.** Convince yourself and your students that they are capable and can do a lot. They can meet and exceed expectation. Set a high bar and regularly tell them that they can get there. SAY what you're thinking when it's positive. They will receive negative feedback much more openly when they know you're on their side and that you believe they can do it better.

IV. **Assess.** Assess your students' learning. Are they where you want them? Is there something they need to get to the next level? Is there something you can do differently?

There are more ways, but those are some starting points.

Study the Steps: The Five Chunks

I suggest following the following outline for each lesson you teach. Most elementary lessons can be organized in what I call the Five Chunks.[4] Here they are:

1. Hello (Opening Activities).
2. Learn 1 (Primary Learning Objective).
3. Wildcard (Change of Pace).
4. Learn 2 (Secondary Learning Objective).
5. Goodbye (Closing Activities).

Each of these Five Chunks will have one or more activities under its heading. For younger students, each activity or song will take 1–2 minutes. For older students, you will do fewer activities and songs and each may take as long as 7 minutes.

In the first chunk, "Hello," you will start your class with joyful opening activities. I sometimes label this section, "Happy Music Time." I recommend having a standard way of starting every class. My opening routine is to start every day with body percussion, sometimes for a minute or two, and sometimes just for 10 seconds. I choose how long based on my objectives and my plan for that day. Then, follow the opening routine with making music together. Plan for mostly familiar songs that will give your students a chance to smile and to participate in something beautiful. This should not be the time when you want them to listen carefully or to get out instruments. Just jump into music-making!

In the second chunk, "Learn 1," you will work on your main music learning objective for that day. For young students this might be keeping a steady beat or finding their singing voice. For older students this might be improvising on just two pitches or practicing music writing. Again, plan for this to take around 5 minutes, and certainly not more than 10.

In the third chunk, "Wildcard," you will do something different. It doesn't matter much what you do, but it must contrast with "Learn 1." If you were up and moving in Learn 1, you will do something seated and quieter for Wildcard. If you were concentrating on figuring out a music notation problem together in Learn 1, you will do an active music game for Wildcard. The main criterion here is "something different!"

The fourth chunk, "Learn 2," will be exactly like Learn 1, but will include your second music learning objective for the day. It's good to contrast your learning objectives so that if Learn 1 is more pitch-based, Learn 2 is more rhythm-based. Or if one includes more singing, the other includes more instrument playing or moving.

The last chunk, "Goodbye," is where you will plan for your closing activities. For younger students, this will include songs that will help bring down the energy level and help them transition to whatever they do after music class. I recommend having a song you always sing as your final song for your youngest students. This signals to them that music time is over and that they will be moving on to the next thing. For older students, this can be a good time to listen to a recording related to the learning they did in class. It can also be a good time for you to perform for them on your main instrument or with your voice. Story songs and ballads are great for this part of the lesson.

What if your music time is particularly long (more than 45 minutes)? Should you just make every section longer? No! These smaller chunks help with students' learning—their brains need a break! Instead, follow the same Five Chunks, but add two more chunks before closing activities: "Learn 3" and a second "Wildcard." These will follow the same model as the previous sections and will still be 5–7 minutes long.

Lesson Outline for Grades 1–6

- Hello (Opening Activities).
  - Opening Routine.
  - Two or three songs that help create a joyful environment.
- Learn 1.
  - An activity or 2–3 songs that meet your primary learning objective.
- Wildcard (Change of Pace).
  - Fun song break.
  - Anything different from the previous and the following sections: worksheet, movement activity, etc.
- Learn 2.
  - An activity or 2–3 songs that meet your secondary learning objective.
- Closing song or activity.

Differences in Teaching Younger and Older Elementary Students

Elementary school spans more ages and stages than any other level of schooling. The differences between a 4-year-old in Pre-K and an 11-year-old in fifth or sixth grade are enormous.

For pre-K, kindergarten, and the first lessons of grade 1, plan several activities with each lasting no more than 3 minutes, and most about 45–65 seconds long. The Five Chunks are modified for these younger students into just three sections:

1. Opening seated music.
2. Standing music.
3. Closing seated music.

Each of these three sections includes 5–10 songs, rhymes, or activities. These younger students generally require more hands-on, involved teaching at the beginning of the year. Chapter 15 is a model for this age group.

For grades 2 and 3, use the Five Chunks and aim for 5- to 7-minute activities, rather than 2- to 3-minute activities. Chapter 16 includes models of what a second and third grade lesson can look like.

For grades 4 and 5, you'll follow a similar outline, but again, give slightly more time for each activity. You might allow them to really work on a problem and spend some time on it. See Chapter 17 for a model.

Each of the model lesson plans in Chapters 15, 16, and 17 is written with many more words than you will use when you teach (or in your own lesson plans). They are written so that you can have enough detail to complete each lesson successfully. You can find the same lessons in outline form in ▶ Appendix C. But you will need to practice them! You'll need very few resources, and I've included all the visual aids and other resources in the appendices and the online supplement. Note that the lessons in Chapters 16 and 17 all include five chunks. If your class time is longer than 30 minutes, you will need to follow the model in those and create your own "Wildcard 2" and "Learn 3" for those lessons. Enjoy the chance for creativity!

Keep in mind that you are absolutely welcomed to make changes in the lessons. But the point is to relieve you of that duty. It is a lot of work making choices about what to include in a lesson and your time is better used by focusing on practicing the lessons rather than thinking about what to include.

Teach Students How to Work in Groups

Set up any group activities with clear instructions and modeling of appropriate group behavior. This is especially important at the beginning of the school year. Here are some things you might say:

- "I will choose a few people for you to work with. This group is just for today and won't be the group you'll have to be in every music class." (Students are generally happier to work with others if you assign the groups).
- "Say, 'Yes!' when someone says their idea, even a small one. Then add to their idea. Create something that *isn't* what you normally would make."
- "Everyone is important in a group. If someone isn't saying much, ask them, "What do you think?"
- "I'm going to walk around and listen for groups that are saying, 'Yes!,' asking questions of each other, and giving encouragement."

In addition, having a clear outline of what groups will do or specific steps for them to complete will make the group time more pleasant for everyone, including you! Write the steps on the board or the screen, for instance:

1. Choose someone to be the scribe, the writer.
2. Brainstorm four ideas of topics for your group (scribe writes them on paper).
3. Ask each person in your group to say something about the ideas.
4. Choose one of the four ideas together.
5. Raise your hand, wait for me, then tell me your choice.

Make clear steps for everything you want them to do that day. As you walk around the classroom, ask each group, "What step are you on?" Encourage students by name and help them get unstuck and to enjoy each other and the activity.

Practice Your Teaching

Good teachers (and good presenters in any field) practice their presentations. It's not enough to have a good plan and to know what you want students to do. You need to practice saying the words aloud, moving around the room, imagining students doing the things you planned for them. Put time into practicing each lesson. Know it so well that you can improvise when things don't go as expected.

Transitions

A good lesson consists of several chunks, as you've seen above. How do you move from one chunk to the next? This is the transition part of your lesson. Some teachers create a story that moves students through each part of the lesson. I recommend not putting much time into planning the transitions, except the time needed to plan the shortest, most concise way to get students to the next thing. A transition could be as simple as finishing one song and immediately saying, "Listen." And singing the next song.

It is generally best to include transitions while students are engaged in something. For instance, you might be doing a song in which students are playing rhythm sticks. When you're ready to move to the next thing, you could say, "As we sing this one last time, please quietly pass your sticks up to me." Then you sing the song while students pass the materials in. When students finish singing, you are ready to go immediately into the next activity—you've eliminated all of the transition time and chaos that would have occurred if you had waited for the song to end and then had them pass in their sticks. This strategy will also help you keep control of your classroom. You want them to be following the fun that you've planned and not creating their own fun (like hitting someone else's sticks or creating a scarecrow with their sticks and their shirt, for instance).

Model More

Music is learned from experiencing music. You are the best model for your students in most situations. If you're teaching a song, you will need to sing it for your students. This will be much more effective and much faster than having them listen to a recording.

Men may need to do some modeling using their falsetto. Children sing an octave higher than most men's natural singing pitch. Navigating that octave displacement is a learned skill for children. They can do it, but it will take some training for them to get there. I recommend using your voice as an instrument, using a neutral syllable to model the pitch, but singing the text of the song in your natural pitch. As an example, you would sing a new song in your natural pitch for your students, then sing it for them again. Then ask them to sing it with you and sing their starting pitch: "Your starting pitch is lu [sung on the starting pitch of the song]." Only the "lu" is sung in falsetto, the rest is spoken.

What about accompanying yourself with an instrument? If you have a piano and can play it, use it! The piano is particularly difficult to use with younger students because it's hard to see them and to communicate nonverbally with them when you're sitting at the piano. If you don't see a way to use it or if you don't play piano, consider using a ukulele, guitar, mountain dulcimer, or autoharp so you can stay close to your students and keep them engaged. These instruments are affordable and easy to pick up without previous experience, at least at a basic level, and they sound good without overpowering the singing of young voices.

Plan to do a lot of singing a cappella, too, so students can hear their voices without accompaniment. This will particularly help in the earliest learning of a song, since they will be able to hear you and see your face and body better than if you're holding or sitting at an instrument.

If students will use an instrument, no matter how simple, model for them how to hold it, what to do when you're not playing, and how to make the sound. Model the correct and the incorrect way to make the sound.

Sing Less

Allow your students to do most of the singing throughout the lesson. As an adult, your voice is not the same timbre as theirs, regardless of your range (bass, tenor, alto, soprano). Allowing them to sing *without you* helps them to develop better singing habits and to avoid trying to sing like you sing. It will also help them grow into confident, independent singers.

Singing less will also benefit you. You will notice your voice tiring this year. Work from the first day to preserve your voice. Speak softly, avoid yelling, and have students sing independently whenever possible.

When you teach a new song, you will need to sing quite a bit; this is modeling. But once students know a song, let them lead it! You might sing just the first few words or first few beats, then drop out inconspicuously.

Singing less is particularly important for anyone who doesn't naturally sing at the same comfortable pitch level as students do. If you are one of these people (as I am), model beautiful singing in your natural pitch, then let students take over.

Pitch matters! Be sure to sing all songs in pitch ranges that students can sing. Neither you nor I enjoy singing outside of our range. Make sure your students don't have to experience that discomfort by choosing appropriate keys for each song. This means using a pitch device (piano, guitar, recorder, tuning fork, or even your phone). Use it every time!

FIGURE 5.1 The suggested range for songs sung at the beginning of the year for students in grades 2 and 3.

FIGURE 5.2 The suggested range for songs sung at the beginning of the year for students in grades 4, 5, and 6.

With students in grades 2 and 3, aim to not go above a D5 (fourth line of the treble staff) and not below a D4 (the D just above middle C), see Figure 5.1.

With students in grades 4, 5, and 6, aim to not go above a D5 (fourth line of the treble staff) and not below a C4 (middle C), see Figure 5.2.

Remember that some of your students will not have much singing experience. It may be initially difficult for them to match pitch. Don't choose a lower starting pitch. Instead, give them grace for now and don't mention it. You can help them find their singing voices by using sirens, using visual aids, using silly voices, and just by having them continue to sing often.

Talk Less

Good teachers know a lot, right? But teachers who talk more are less likely to teach well. Instead of talking, do! Show your students, model, have students model, ask a better question (see "Ask Better Questions"). Keep your words few. I ask my college students to teach a 7-minute lesson using no more than ten words. They write the ten words they will use on the board, then teach their lesson using only those. Though I don't think teachers need to be that extreme in their day-to-day teaching, I do think my students come away with knowing that they can teach with less talking (and what the important words to use are!). For example, if I am about to use a rhyme with young students about a bee I can say:

"Ok, kids. This next rhyme is about a bee. Have any of you ever seen a bee before? I know I have. I remember one time when my friend kicked a beehive—yikes! We had to get out of there fast! Listen to this rhyme about bees."

Or I can just say:

"Listen."

Just one word instead of forty-seven! I think the reason people use more words is because they want students to like the rhyme and they think that by saying a lot about it they can influence students to like the rhyme or song. Or it could just be nerves! Some people talk more when they're nervous. Either way, students will respond better with fewer words. The fewer words you use, the more time can be spent with the music! Just saying, "Listen," moves students directly into the rhyme. They can enjoy it as it is and enjoy it more the next time you say it, then the most when they get to say the rhyme.

Aim for as few words as possible. Plan your words, plan how you will introduce the next activity and practice it!

Ask Better Questions

Think about your questions: What answers might students give? Do your questions naturally lead toward the thing you want students to know? Questions for the sake of questions are boring and will lead to students not paying attention and losing interest. Instead, carefully select which questions you will use and what objectives they meet.

One reason I use questions is to help students learn a rhyme or song more quickly. My objective is their memory, so my questions lead them to remember the rhyme or song. Here is one rhyme I used with early elementary students:

Bee, bee, bumblebee.
Stung a man upon his knee.
Stung a pig upon his snout.
I declare that you are out.[5]

The questions I use are, in this order:

- What insect is in this rhyme? (A bee)
- Who does the bee sting first? Next? (A man and a pig)
- Where does the bee sting the man? The pig? (The man on his knee and the pig on his snout)
- What is a snout? Can you show me? (A pig's nose, students point to their noses)

I follow these questions by saying, "Let's say this rhyme together. Pat with me." Then we all pat the beat and say the rhyme. Notice that each of these questions follows naturally from the previous question and leads students to think through the rhyme in order. Also, note that each question meets the objective of helping students remember the rhyme. The questions lead to understanding the rhyme and thus remembering it. These are in contrast to questions that will elicit a response from students, but that might lead away from my objectives for this activity:

Have you ever been stung by a bee?
How many of you have seen a bee?
How do you feel when a bee lands on you?

There is nothing wrong with these questions, but they will probably encourage younger students to respond with more energy and for them to feel as though they are about to be stung by a bee right then (they are excellent pretenders!). This might be acceptable for later in a lesson, but not when my focus is on steady beat.

In short, decide on your questions ahead of time. Use only questions that meet your objectives for that lesson and that bring students along the path you have prepared for them.

Listen More

You are a good musician! You can sing songs beautifully and play instruments accurately. But your students are just learning. They won't sound as polished. The natural reaction to this is to sing when students are singing to make the whole group sound better (at least to you). Or to play instruments with your students so that they can follow you and they will sound better. Don't fall for it! Instead of singing or playing an instrument with your students, model it and listen to what they do. If they're not performing as you'd like, model it again using a positive and a negative model. Again, avoid singing while they are singing. This will allow you to listen to them and to how they are singing.

Make eye contact with your students throughout your lesson. You need to know how they are responding. Remind yourself to look each child in the eye several times throughout the lesson. Are there students you find you're always looking at? Probably so. Students who give lots of nonverbal feedback, nodding when you say something or smiling to show their understanding, will naturally get more attention from you. You will have to work to check in with quieter students and those who are more reserved.

Students grow best when they are getting appropriate feedback from a teacher who hears them and who tailors instruction to what they are doing. Listening to students (rather than performing on instruments or singing with them) allows you to be a coach pushing them to better things. You're not hiding their sound with your own, professional sound.

Reflect on Your Teaching

Your first day is not too early to be thinking of becoming a better teacher (more on this in Chapter 11). For now, be kind to yourself, know that you will get better, and do a quick reflection at the end of each day. You don't need to do a formal, written reflection, just ask yourself questions like the following:[6]

Did I see all of my students?
Did I model and listen? (Instead of singing or playing with my students)
Did I use prepared, concise questions?
What did I do well?
What do I need to work on?
What parts of my lesson need more practice?

Conclusion

What you do and don't do will help develop the climate and expectations for your classroom. Speak less, sing less, listen more. Invite students to speak more, sing more, and listen more. You will spend a lot of time preparing for teaching. This is the hard part—the fun will come! Like a farmer who sows seed in one season and harvests crops in another season, your reward will come!

Checklist for Preparing Your Lessons

- ☐ Find a way to remind yourself to be positive and kind each you meet with a class, especially those that are difficult (perhaps a sign in your room, a piece of jewelry you will wear when you teach, a routine you will follow each day, or writing a positive reminder to yourself in your lesson plans).
- ☐ Read and study each of the lessons in Chapters 15 and 16. If you're not teaching all of the grades, just read the chapters appropriate to you.
- ☐ Work through the lists in each of those chapters.
- ☐ Make sure the people close to you know that you will have a lot of work these first few weeks.
- ☐ Make a plan for practicing your teaching, actually saying the words out loud that you will say in your lesson. When will you do this? Where? How long will it take?
- ☐ Write into your planner or calendar time for reflection on your teaching. Write questions that you'd like to ask yourself after you teach a class (or at the end of each day). Or used the suggested questions in the section "Reflect on Your Teaching" earlier in this chapter.

Checklist for Preparing to Teach Any Lesson

- ☐ Read the objectives and remember what you're hoping students will get out of the lesson.
- ☐ Gather the materials required for the lesson, including anything you need to print, copy, or make.
- ☐ Review all the songs so that you can sing them confidently without looking at the notation.
- ☐ Read through the lesson at least twice, making notes of things you want to remember to do and things you need to get. You can substitute rhymes and songs, but make it easy on yourself.
- ☐ Reduce the lesson to an outline form, or use the outline format provided in the supplemental materials on the OUP website.
- ☐ Consider reducing the lesson to a sticky note or notecard, especially for your youngest students. This is what you will teach from and will help remind you of what is next in your lesson.

PART II

After Week Three

Building Excitement, Building Routines

6

Design Lessons That Lead to Learning

Introduction

Teaching a lesson plan and creating a lesson plan are two separate skills. In the previous chapter, you considered how to teach a lesson well, so that students would learn. In this chapter, you will make plans for how you will create your own lessons for your students. It is likely that you have created and taught some successful lessons in your life. This chapter will refresh your memory on designing lessons and help you focus on what is most important for you right now.

Choosing Activities

How do you choose which activities to give to which grades? In general, if an activity is appropriate and fun for multiple levels, I will save it for the oldest level that will love it. My teacher and mentor, Susan Brumfield, calls this the "Disneyland Principle."[1] The idea is to give your students things they will love and enjoy, but giving them small joys that grow incrementally into larger ones.

Picture taking your kids to Disneyland. Of course, they will enjoy it at any age, but parks don't get much better than that, and it might make future, lesser parks less enjoyable for them. Instead, if they are very excited about going to the playground down the street, go there! Then, raise the excitement by going to a bigger playground in a nearby neighborhood, then an even bigger playground. When you go to a small, local amusement park, your children's excitement will be through the roof! Then maybe a carnival, etc., but saving the best for later as much as possible.

This kind of incremental increasing of fun gives your children, perhaps, the most joy possible. Each new park brings something better than what they've ever experienced.

Your First Year as an Elementary Music Teacher. Andrew S. Paney, Oxford University Press. © Oxford University Press 2025.
DOI: 10.1093/oso/9780197631430.003.0006

Rather than depriving them of Disneyland, you're giving them joy at more parks than they would have had in a different order. It's about comparisons.

Certainly, some games can be used in multiple grades, but you do run the risk of older students rejecting a game they would actually enjoy because, "That's a baby game."

There are several sources of musical games, and I mention a few at the end of this chapter. Singing games are great ways to increase fun and improve singing and musical sense (especially rhythm) in your students. I've included sources that are available online for free or purchase.[2] There are *many* other good resources, but my aim is to give you a good start, not to list every good book or website.

Planning Long-Term

What do you want your oldest students to know and be able to do by the time they leave you? Even better, what do you want them to be able to do when they graduate high school and how can each prior experience lead to that point? If you can work with other teachers to make that happen, you will have an excellent program in your district.

That can be difficult to do, especially in your first year. For now, focus on what you want your students to be able to do by the time they leave you. If you teach K-5, for example, what skills do you want your fifth grade students to be able to have at the end of the year? Work backward from there to plan what each grade will accomplish. What skills will they need to have in fourth grade to get to that point? Third grade? Second? First? Kindergarten? Now you have a curriculum.

The problem is that your fifth graders this year will probably not have had music, or at least they won't have had music with you. This activity will really help you the most with your younger students, your K, 1, and 2 students. You will be preparing yourself for good musical experiences a few years into your teaching career.

But what do you do with your older students? I suggest starting with the skills presented in the section under the heading "What Do You Want Them to Do?" Don't write those students off—help them to learn! Fifth grade students (ages 10 and 11, usually) are in a time of incredible brain growth. They will benefit from the things you teach them for the rest of their lives. And they won't benefit from things you don't teach them. Make it count!

What Do You Want Them to Know?

Many elementary music classes overemphasize musical knowledge: composers, eras, dates, clefs, staff note names, rhythms names, etc. I encourage you to focus on the *doing* of music. In an elementary art class, for example, students draw and paint and color and fold, They don't spend most of their time learning history, specific techniques, or art vocabulary. They *do* art! In the same way, we can give students the musical *skills* to be able to do music independently at a deeper level.

What Do You Want Them to Do?

What musical skills will you develop in your students? This question is particularly important in the music room. This is not about what activities you want them to accomplish each class session, but rather deciding which skills you want them to develop over their time with you. What knowledge and skills do you want students to gain? This starts with your oldest students. Make some decisions about how you want them to grow in their musical skills, mentioned first in Chapter 5:

Reading.
Writing.
Creating (improvising and composing).
Singing.
Playing instruments.
Moving (body movement including conducting and dancing).
Listening.
Audiating.
Memorizing.

The NCAS asks teachers to instruct students of all ages in these areas. I believe all musicians, even those far beyond college-age, should be developing all of these skills throughout their lives. But for now, decide what level you want your students to reach by the end of their time with you. What should they be able to read in terms of rhythms? What about pitches? What creating experiences do you want them to be successful at when they leave you? What do you want their singing to sound like? And so on.

Getting Started with the National Core Arts Standards (NCAS)

The NCAS were developed to align all of the arts disciplines (dance, media arts, music, theater, and visual arts) with similar objectives throughout a child's education. Experts in each arts discipline met together to work out an overall framework and to fill in specific details unique to each arts area. They organized arts learning into four practices: Creating, Performing/Producing/Presenting, Responding, and Connecting. All music teachers already help their students grow in each of these practices. And the standards make the goals for each grade-level for each of these practices clear.

The codes with multiple numbers and letters are not difficult to decipher. Each code lets you know the discipline, which learning practice is addressed, the specific standard, and the grade level. In Figure 6.1, for example:

- MU" refers to the discipline. This is a Music standard.
- "Re" refers to the practice. This is a Responding standard.

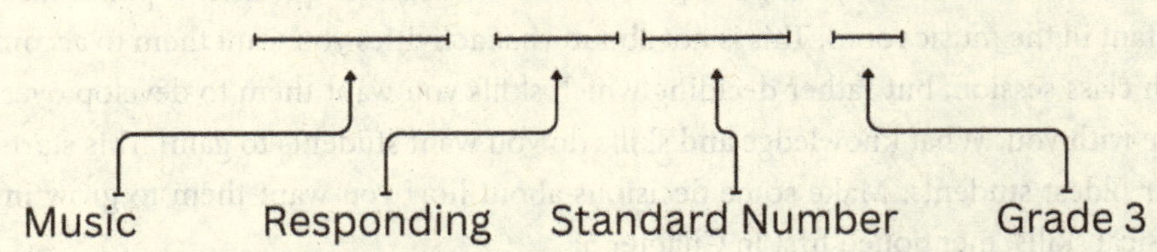

FIGURE 6.1 Understanding the National Core Arts Standards (NCAS) codes.

- The first numbers, "7.1" identify the particular standard.[3]
- The final number, "3," indicates the grade. This is a grade 3 standard.

Though the standards are easy to find online, it can be difficult to understand and use them effectively. Here is how I recommend starting your relationship with the NCAS:

a. Go to https://www.nationalartsstandards.org/ and select "Customize your own handbook." Make the appropriate selections for your teaching situation. I recommend being as narrow as possible, selecting the fewest possible boxes to represent your teaching position.
b. For Disciplines, you'll select "Music" and "Music (PK-8)."
c. For Practices, select all four options.
d. For Grades, select only the grades you will teach.
e. Select "EUs and EQs" and "Process Components."
f. Save your handbook by clicking the "Download Your Handbook" button. Then move the document to your mobile device or print it out for yourself.
g. Make a date with your handbook. Go get a coffee or put up a hammock in a park and take only your handbook, a highlighter (or highlighting mobile app), and a drink. Plan to spend just 30–45 minutes reading through the paragraphs introducing the NCAS and a few of the actual standards (the sentences with lots of letters and numbers in front of them, e.g., MU:Cr2.1.2.a). Note that the words themselves will probably take 10–15 minutes, but you may want to spend some time comparing different grades and skill areas.
h. Don't panic. It's not especially easy reading material. If there's something you don't understand or if you start to feel overwhelmed, just take a break and come back to it later. You do *not* have to master them in one day, you'll have a long relationship together!
i. Consider the standards as a consultant in your process. As you make your lesson plans, take a look for the standards that relate to the activity you're planning.

j. First, just ask yourself which of the main categories your activity fits under: Creating, Performing/Producing/Presenting, Responding, or Connecting.
k. Then, look up the two or three Anchor Standards that are included under that practice (search "what are the creating anchor standards for music?").
l. Finally, open up your standards and look for the grade level you're planning for.
m. When you've done just these few things, you will know four parts of the standard you're looking for (arts discipline, practice, Anchor Standard, and grade). This will significantly reduce the number of standards to read through and will allow you to read those two or three possible standards carefully and slowly. Choose the standard that best fits and allow that standard to inform how you do your plan.
n. Tighten up your lesson as you check in on the standards and go back and forth.

Work Backward

Once you know what you want your oldest students to be able to do, move backward to what they need to know before they get to those places. Create your curriculum with that end point in mind.

You can find some sample curricula at the sources below. Your music teaching situation will likely be different from those used in the planning of these curricula, but they will give you an idea of what students are able to do at each grade level.

1. Music Will, musicwill.org. This organization works with teachers and schools to provide music lessons and resources, focusing on a modern band approach. There is no fee to use the materials on their website.
2. MusicplayOnline, musicplayonline.com. This site offers lesson plans that are ready to go for your classroom. There is a monthly or yearly fee, but you can peruse some resources free to see if it is something that will work for you.
3. Aileen's Music Room, mrsmiraclesmusicroom.com. This site includes full lesson plans for the entire year for grades 1–3. These are available for a fee and include the materials for activities, too. You can find many other similar sites by searching online.

Physical, Mental, and Emotional Growth

Elementary-aged students change and grow quickly, both physically and in their behavior and knowledge. You will notice that first graders are very different from second graders, and second from third, etc. The changes are often much more pronounced than those of adults or students in secondary schools.

A rewarding part of teaching elementary music is how much students can learn and how well they can learn it. It's easy to underestimate how much students can do and know at young ages. This will become clearer as you teach and spend time with younger children. The important part is this: plan for the diverse level of achievement of students in each of your grades. You can't ask someone to do a task that they physically or mentally or emotionally can't do. And you don't want to ask someone to do something that doesn't give them some challenge. The challenge is where the fun is. Children often like puzzles (or even video games) because they challenge them and make them do things that are difficult, but attainable. They believe they will be able to achieve the desired result, but it takes work to get there. That is the enjoyable part of it.

Long-Range Planning

For now, focus on the first three weeks of class. Later, it will help to know how far you can take your students. I recommend writing a **Long Range Plan** for what you want your students to have learned once they graduate onto the next level. Then, decide which things you will teach at each grade to meet that objective. This will give you your **Yearly Plan**. Finally, create **Unit Plans** for each curricular item you want to cover. Having these will make your **Daily Lesson Plan** writing much easier. This may seem like a lot of decisions to make, but remember that you're not locked into whatever you choose—this will change throughout your career. You will become a better teacher and see things differently. Count on it!

Daily Lesson Plans

In each lesson plan you will have the following sections, in this order (see this modeled in Chapters 15, 16, and 17):

- Objectives.
- Materials.
- Songs and Other Music.
- National Standards.
- Procedures.

The Objectives are the main things you want students to take away from the lesson. If someone were to ask you why you were doing a particular activity in this lesson, your answer should be something like, "My objective for this lesson was _____ and that activity helps students to meet that objective."

The Materials are everything you need to have available for the lesson to occur. It includes classroom materials (whiteboard, markers, pencils, papers) as well as specific visual aids and recordings. The Songs and Other Music section lists the songs you may need to review and recordings you may need to locate.

In the National Standards section, list the specific standards you are aiming to address in the lesson. See "Getting Started with The National Core Arts Standards (NCAS)" above.

In Procedures, you will list the activities and give yourself some reminders about how to deliver the lesson. In the last chapters of this book, you'll see detailed procedures. They are so detailed, in fact, that they may be difficult to teach from. The point is to give you a clear picture of what happens in the lesson. Appendix C includes the same lessons, but reduced to an outline form that you can easily teach from.

5 to 7 Minutes

A big part of pacing your lessons well is knowing how long your students can stay on one activity. I suggest you aim for each part of your lesson to take between 5 and 7 minutes. This means, for a 35-minute lesson, you would have five, six, or seven different activities. For a 50-minute lesson, you would have seven to ten activities. Though some students can focus for a longer period of time, most or all of your students can learn in 5- to 7-minute spans of time.[4]

Each of these 5- to 7-minute sections will have a musical objective and will allow and encourage students to delight in the work that they're doing and have a great, overall experience.

Choose Contrasting Activities

As you choose activities for your sections, plan to contrast your activities so students experience multiple modes of learning. This will help their learning, help with classroom management, and be more fun for you and for the students. For example, a lesson that begins with singing, might follow with rhythm work. A lesson with a writing activity might proceed to a singing game. This will help the most students to thrive in your class.

Pace Your Lessons for Success and Delight

Transitions between these sections are where you can lose time and the attention of the children. Your class will move much more smoothly when you master your transitions. As I've worked with developing teachers it has become clear that this takes a lot of work, even when you think you've got it!

Transitions require a balance between keeping attention and building connections. Reducing the time of your transitions will help students stay on task, avoid talking, and reduce the opportunity for disruptions of any sort. Extremely short transitions, less than 2 seconds, may help with keeping students' attention and reducing distraction. Classrooms where there is excessive talking and where the teacher regularly has to call the students back to order usually suffer from dead air; the teacher has not planned or practiced their transitions. The difficult part is thinking of how you start the next section of your lesson while the current section is still progressing. This takes practice.

Transitions can also be used to build rapport with and to get to know your students. You can facilitate this by using transition times to share about the music, to ask questions of students, and to draw connections to other outside-of-music curricula. There are many ways you can build those connections as you transition into or out of a song or piece of music. You could (1) encourage students to think about how someone might feel while listening to a particular piece of music, (2) tell a personal story about why you chose the music or why the text is significant to you, or (3) create a fictional story that connects the two activities or songs. There are many more ways you can use transitions to get to know your students and to build community within a class. Try some approaches and see how they work for you.

Plan Extension Activities

As a new teacher, it's easy to overestimate how long an activity will take students. Count on it! It will happen to you as it happens to everyone. Instead of being left surprised, make a plan for what you will do if your lesson runs short. Some options for you are to:

Have some fun, individual worksheets available for students to do. These could be crossword puzzles, word finds, word scrambles, or other puzzles or games. The only criteria I would suggest are: (1) it is self-sufficient, giving them all they need to know on the sheet, including directions (2) it is fun enough for them to be glad to do it.

Choose a game that you wouldn't otherwise have time to include. A game like Rhythm Baseball or Rhythm Basketball (described in Chapters 13 and 14) is a great way to fill up some time with older students.

Redo a musical activity or game that they did in a previous class. I like to have a record of songs and games they have completed so I can suggest a few. It works well to have them choose one, too. You can offer two or three activities or songs and have them vote, letting them know up front that you will do the one with the most votes. This gives them some ownership and some commitment to the activity (not to mention taking up a little of the extra time you're trying to fill!).

Listening to a piece of music can be effective at this point in the lesson. They probably are calmer than they were at the beginning of the lesson and open to listening to something, even something unfamiliar. The lessons in Chapter 16 and 17 give a model of how listening might fit into the end of a listening lesson.

Checklist for Designing Successful Lessons

- ☐ Read the lessons in Chapter 15, 16, or 17 from the top to the bottom without judging or thinking about how you would do it.
- ☐ Write out the lessons in bullets for yourself.
- ☐ Practice the lessons as they are and make notes about what works and doesn't work for you.
- ☐ If the lesson includes song you don't know, change them to ones you do.
- ☐ Make a plan for how you will practice the lesson.
- ☐ Later, consider what skills you would like for your older students to leave with and work backward to your planning.
- ☐ Spend some time reading others' lesson plans, both published and unpublished.

7

Choose Songs That Work

Introduction

One particularly challenging task for a music teacher is finding appropriate songs to teach in class. Of course, there are many kinds of music you will use in your room: recordings, instrumental arrangements, multimedia events, and more. But none of these has the same cost to you if it doesn't work for your students. Teaching a song is a time-intensive task because it involves so many parts:

- Searching the literature,
- Choosing the song,
- Deciding where the song would fit best,
- Learning the song,
- Planning how to teach the song,
- Then, finally, teaching the song to your students.

Of these six steps, the fourth is often the most underestimated.

Where Do You Start?

Here is a pop quiz for you. Please actually write an answer for each of these questions—it will help you understand this chapter much better and get more from it. You can write it here in the book, on a piece of paper, or even on your mobile device.

1. What is a song that your parents or caregivers sang for you when you were a young child?
2. Name three songs you sang or might sing with your own children when they were or are very young?

Your First Year as an Elementary Music Teacher. Andrew S. Paney, Oxford University Press. © Oxford University Press 2025.
DOI: 10.1093/oso/9780197631430.003.0007

3. What is a song you sang as a child that has very few words? Is there one that someone who doesn't speak your language could probably learn?

Did you answer those? Here are my answers:

"Jesus Loves Me," "Twinkle, Twinkle, Little Star"

"Jesus Loves Me," "Twinkle, Twinkle, Little Star," "The Alphabet Song," "Firefly, Firefly," and "Old MacDonald Had a Farm."

"Mary Had a Little Lamb," "London Bridge Is Falling Down," "Bingo" and "Row Row Row Your Boat."

The songs I remember my parents singing to me are songs I sing with my children now. Songs have a long life and they seem to make up a part of our identity as people. This is a powerful responsibility, when students may remember songs they sing with you into their adulthood!

Are the songs you learned nontraditional? That's OK! Did you grow up in a non-English-speaking country—great! Use simple songs from your childhood, in the original language, and teach them by rote. Young students, in particular, will respond well and enjoy the uniqueness. Do you expect all of your students will already know the songs you know? They might, but it's likely many of them won't.

I learned perhaps all of the songs in my list by rote, from someone who cared about me. I sang all of them countless times and I could sing them now without having to practice or review the words. Learning a new song, though, is difficult for me (and can be for any music teacher). We can read music well and actually learn it quickly, too. Plus, the songs we're teaching our students are simple, right?! Then why is it so tough to learn new songs well enough to teach them?

I suggest you start with songs you already know: songs you learned in school, on the playground, from family, and from your music training. This will help you avoid having to learn multiple new songs at once. Make a list of the ones you know and decide which ages will enjoy singing them. It's likely that many songs can be used over multiple age groups.

Singing these songs that you know will help you to connect with your students, to share something personal about yourself, and will reduce the amount of preparation time you will need at the beginning of the year.

Once you've used all the songs you already know, you will need to start learning some other songs. The best way to learn new songs is to learn them from another person. Go to music teacher workshops in your area to learn some new songs you can use quickly. Music education conferences (state, regional, national, and international) can be a great place to learn new songs, too. Learning songs in these contexts accelerates the learning process significantly and allows you to learn many more songs without the additional work required to learn from a printed copy of a song. See "A Strategy for Learning a New Song" for more help.

Know Your Community

Because of the power of music, you can bring joy to your community and pride to your students as you make *their* music relevant and prevalent. Children from a minority community do not necessarily even know they're from a minority community. They may see that the music their family sings or listens to is not present anywhere else, but they may not think anything of it—that's just the way the world is! When you sing one of *their* songs, you will see their faces light up with recognition at something they have never experienced and never even dreamed was possible. You've given them the gift of acknowledgment and affirmation of who they are.

How do you do this? Be kind, talk to parents, ask them about their music: what they sing, what they listen to. Ask them the same questions you answered at the beginning of this chapter.

Try to do some research on your own and ask them: "Do you know this song?" And then ask them to sing it for you. Ask them what songs they sing to babies and what songs they remember singing when they were growing up. Ask them if there are songs that you might be able to teach in your classroom, perhaps songs with few words.

Songs That Harm and Songs That Heal

Music is powerful. That is the reason you and I got into this field in the first place—we felt something and wanted to do it more. Music has power to move people. For this reason, many songs come out of times, both culturally and personally, when people are feeling deep emotions: love, hate, longing, loss, joy, sorrow, regret, etc. Some songs that meant a lot to people did so at the expense of other people. Some songs were written that did not mean a lot to anybody, but were very harmful to some.

What is our responsibility as music teachers in the area of song selection? We have a limited amount of time with students, so we can use that time to present them a very selective repertoire of music that represents what we believe to be the best. A song that can cause emotional pain to someone else does not necessarily need to be deleted forever, but it does not need to be in the relatively small number of works your students will receive from you.

At the time of the writing of this book, there is a lot of talk about song selection in schools.[1] You may have strong feelings about this topic and if you do, you probably already have criteria for choosing and omitting songs. If you haven't thought about this much before, I recommend giving some thought to the songs that you use in your lessons. Again, you can only present a few works and songs in the school year because your time is limited.[2]

If a parent or student objects to a song you've chosen, in general, I recommend finding another one. It is a lot of work to try to defend your choice and it's unlikely that you will convince someone. It also is good general practice to avoid songs that you know will cause controversy.

How do you know if a song will potentially cause trouble? First, it's easy to see that songs that include offensive language should be avoided. This includes expletives and words that refer to an ethnic group that people from that group would not embrace.[3] Also, you may want to avoid songs with subject matter that may be sensitive like death, sex, and violence. It becomes clearer and clearer why so many children's songs are about animals!

What songs heal? The music that may make a difference in your students' lives is music that values them and their families. It means a great deal to a student who feels like an outsider when a teacher acknowledges their story, their experience, and their music. Do some research on your community and find out what communities are represented at your school. If your area has a large number of Arabic families, search online for Arabic children's songs. If you have a lot of Peruvian families, look for Peruvian songs. This may require a little bit more research on your part to find specific songs from particular people groups in that country. Also, keep in mind that even though you found a song from someone's country doesn't guarantee that they will know that song or even recognize it.

Apart from online and library research, perhaps your best resource will be people in your community. I recommend starting with the teachers and administrators in your building. Ask them a question like, "What songs do you think most of our students sing when they are young?" Or "How would I find information about the songs most of these students would know from their early childhood?" As you get to know your students and their parents, you will build trust enough to ask parents about songs they sing with their children or songs they sing to babies. And once you've gathered this information, you will be able to share it with teachers in other schools through a blog or a conference presentation. Your work can benefit lots of teachers and even more students as you share what you discover.

Choosing Songs for Younger Students

Younger students, before they reach third grade, tend to be very open to music and songs that are different from the ones they're accustomed to. Of course, some older students are, too, but in the younger grades majority of the class is likely to respond well to almost any music you present to them. This means that almost any song you know will work and be successful with these younger students. For me, this has meant choosing songs that I will save for older students, since they can be trickier to choose for.

Choosing Songs for Older Students

Older students in grades 3 through 6, can be a bit more selective about songs. They may be skeptical of the music you present to them (in the same way that we as adults are often skeptical of music with which we are not familiar). These students, in particular, do not want to do "baby" music. They are discovering their own preferences and want to be respected. Songs that have a surprise or a twist or that are funny (to them, not to you) can be big hits with these students.

Choosing Songs for a Performing Group

You do not need to purchase choral octavos for a beginning choir. Instead, follow the same procedures detailed above. It's great to do unison pieces with a young choir. You can take simple, short folksongs from any culture and create performance works of them together with your students. Talk about introductions, then create one together. Talk about codas, then create one together. Talk about accompaniments, talk about pedal tones or ostinatos, talk about rounds—you get the idea. Aim for the pieces you create and select to be about two minutes long.

It is absolutely OK to teach music by rote with your performing groups. Until you develop their reading skills, you will not have a better option! Focus on other musical skills when you teach something by rote. Ask them to experiment with dynamics, with expression, with their sound or tone quality or timbre. Ask, "This time, I'd like you to sing this like you're in first grade." "Now, sing it like you're in sixth grade." "What did you like about the second sound? Which do you think we should use for this song?" Explore the musical options together and aim for a beautiful performance that students are proud to share with their families.

A Strategy for Learning a New Song

I think learning a new song is one of the toughest parts of being a music teacher. As a teacher, you need to really know something before you teach it. Here is how I approach for learning a new song or rhyme myself and how I ask my students to do it:

1. READ the rhyme ten times to yourself aloud. Try to picture what the words are talking about and really engage with what is happening. Can you add hand or body motions? If you do, it will be easier for you and for your students! Add the motions in this step and use them EVERY time in the next steps.
2. SAY the rhyme ten times by memory aloud. It's OK to peek back at the words, but try to be away from the words by the sixth time. Don't rush, just enjoy each time and try using different voices.
3. Take a break of about 1–2 minutes. Don't think about the rhyme, but just take a short walk, get a drink, or check your phone.
4. READ the rhyme three times again. Really look at each word.
5. SAY the rhyme three times by memory again, trying not to peek.
6. SAY the rhyme ten times by memory again, using different voices (high, low, grandma, lumberjack, Donald Duck, etc.) and different speeds.
7. Take another break.
8. Say it four more times by memory and YOU'RE DONE!

Some tips for learning:

- Just do it! Go straight down the list of eight steps above without second guessing yourself. It's hard work! Don't be discouraged, just keep to the steps.
- Set a timer if you'd like—this can really help if you're feeling discouraged. Set it for 4 minutes, then take a short break. Repeat until you finish all eight steps!
- REMEMBER: The rhymes and songs for young students are generally very short, just 8–12 seconds. Saying a rhyme ten times only takes about 2 minutes.

This looks like a long process, but each step doesn't take very long. Stick with it and it will pay off.

Teaching a New Song

Here is a way to teach a new song to students (rhymes follow the same process). There are lots of ways to do this, and the song you're teaching will have a large effect on the best way to teach it. Consider this a starting point and try it out. Here are the four steps:

1. OVERVIEW—Teacher sings the song two times alone.
2. BREAK IT DOWN—Teacher asks questions that lead toward memory and understanding of the song.
3. REPEAT WITH VARIATION—Teacher and students say rhyme together, repeating it several times with variation each time (faster or slower, in a higher or lower pitch, or with added hand motions, for example).
4. ASSESSMENT—Students perform the song alone (or teacher visually and aurally checks for learning).

Some notes about this process:

- Always have the song memorized before you teach it. Never read it—you want to make it engaging!
- The students may enjoy keeping the beat with you, even when they are not singing with you.
- If your song has hand or body motions, have the students do motions with you from the beginning of your teaching, if applicable.
- Step 2 should be students responding to specific questions the teacher asks. The purpose is for them to understand the song, so that they will memorize it more quickly.
- In step 3, the variations allow the students to repeat the song many times without tiring of it. Think of comparative concepts (high/low, same/different, loud/soft, fast/slow).
- Try to get the students to sing the song alone without knowing they're doing it alone.

Checklist for Choosing Songs

☐ Create a list of songs you already know well. You can start your list by answering the three questions at the beginning of this chapter:

- What is a song that your parents or caregivers sang for you when you were a young child?
- Name three songs you sang with your own children when they were very young. Alternatively, choose songs you might choose to sing with young children, from babies through age 4.
- What is a song you sang as a child that has very few words? Is there one that someone who doesn't speak your language could probably learn?

Once you have an initial list:

☐ Note on your list the songs that would be appropriate for each grade you will teach (e.g., pre-K, K, first, second, etc.).

☐ Later, move your list into three separate song lists: early elementary, intermediate, and upper elementary. Write the name of each song you want to use with each grade, remembering that you can use the same song on more than one list.

☐ Evaluate your list: How many game songs are on your list? How many story songs? How many rhymes? How many major, minor, and modal songs? How many duple or triple meter songs? What genres of songs are included (work songs, lullabies, waltzes)? Make a note of which categories need additional songs for each of your three lists.

In the Future

☐ Ask teachers you know (both music teachers and classroom teachers) a question like, "What songs do you think most of our students sing when they are young?" Or "How would I find information about the songs most of these students would know from their early childhood?"

☐ Make a plan to ask students about songs they sing with their families or that they remember from when they were very young.

☐ Make a plan to ask students' parents the same questions you answered at the beginning of this chapter.

Checklist for Evaluating the Fit of a New Song

☐ Write down what kind of a song you want, answering these questions:
- What grade level are you targeting?
- Is there a topic or subject you'd like to include?
- Do you want it to be a song that students sing or just listen to?
- If students will sing it, what range should it have?

☐ Once you've answered these questions, consult some sources:
- Start with yourself: Do you know a song that fits your criteria?
- Then consult trusted online sources.
- Ask other music teachers you know or look for an appropriate social media group. Be sure to include the answers to the questions above (for example, "I'm looking for a song about transportation (especially trains) for my second grade students to sing. I'd prefer something in minor and compound meter if possible. Do you have any ideas of songs that might be a good fit? Thanks in advance!"

☐ Once you have found a song that you think might work, remind yourself that music is a powerful art form and it will have an effect on your students. Ask yourself:
- Do I think this is a good song?
- Does it have language that could be offensive (expletives, racial slurs)?
- Does it have references to violence, death, crimes, or sex?
- Would this song be one that older elementary students could grow to enjoy (i.e., not too young for them)?

☐ Now work on learning the song!

8

Plan Concerts and Programs

Why Give a Program or Performance?

A concert or a program can be a great way to help you meet your objectives for your students. In a program, you can show teachers, administrators, and parents what your students know and can build support for what you want the music at the school to be. As you begin this chapter, think about what you would like to accomplish through a program. What is your overall objective for your students? How can a concert move them toward that objective?

A pitfall of concerts and programs is that they can become ends in themselves and can take away from what students can learn through regular music instruction. You can avoid this mistake by keeping your objectives in mind from the planning stage through the end of the school year. Instead of pursuing a flawless, touching, awe-inspiring concert, consider how you can use the performance and preparation time to give your students:

A taste of performing.
A chance to show what they are learning.
A product in which they can take pride.
A memorable musical moment.

Beauty can (and should) be a part of this performance, but perfection probably shouldn't be.

Which Students Give Programs?

Think about the structure of your school and what you can manage with the time you have. If you teach K through sixth grade, it is unreasonable to think that you could present

Your First Year as an Elementary Music Teacher. Andrew S. Paney, Oxford University Press. © Oxford University Press 2025.
DOI: 10.1093/oso/9780197631430.003.0008

seven different performances each year. There are two solutions to this: combine classes or choose some grades that will always include a performance.

If you have a smaller school, a school with three or fewer classes per grade, you may be able to combine grades for a performance. For instance, you might have three performances: K–1, 2–3, and 4–5. That is a reasonable number to do in a year. I recommend *not* doing them all on the same night, but perhaps doing the 2–3 concert in December, the 4–5 concert in early March, and the K–1 concert in May. This particular arrangement would allow your younger students to have the most time for growth, but still give your older students something to work toward for most of the year.

For many, a set plan for performances may be the best option. Plan for only grades 1, 3, and 5 to give a performance each year. Students in K, 2, and 4 will focus only on the curriculum. This plan allows for every student to be in a program and for parents and teachers to know when they can expect a program from children. If you do this, it would be nice to have the students performing for those who are not performing at least once during the year. This allows all students to have a chance to be an audience member and a performer regularly throughout their elementary career. Having a plan like this also allows other teachers to plan for events, too. Another teacher may want to do something special with students only in the years they aren't performing, for instance, the art teacher could do art shows with students in grades K, 2, and 4. Parents may appreciate the care that you can put into these performances and will probably be glad to have fewer commitments.

What to Include in a Program

For now, avoid looking for a published program. I think you will find that tailoring your program to your students is much simpler than trying to find the perfect published program. You will need to spend several hours researching and testing published programs to find the right fit. And even when you do, you may find that it is more (or less) than you expected: it may be too difficult, too easy, too long, too short, and it even may require more resources that you anticipate in terms of instruments, props, or set design.

Instead, create your program using music you're already doing in your classes. Choose a theme and make the songs and musical selections you've used in the classroom fit that theme. A possible theme for a young elementary program would be "A Day at the Zoo," or "The Farm Wakes Up." For either of these themes, you would include five to seven songs and rhymes that have animals in them. You could also write narration parts to be read by students (or their teachers, depending on your situation and objective). For example:

> **Narrator**: Old MacDonald woke up one morning and thought, I need to get to work!
>
> **Students** sing "Old MacDonald Had a Farm" and use a lamb as their first animal.[1]

Narrator: Old MacDonald's daughter Mary was taking care of her sweet, little friend.

Students sing "Mary Had a Little Lamb"

Narrator: After feeding Mary's lamb, Old MacDonald went down to the pig pen. The pig was excited to get his first meal, so excited that . . .

Students say "To Market" rhyme (To market, to market / To buy a fat pig / Home again, home again / Jiggity jig).[2]

The narration and weaving the story will still make for a very short program. The next section gives ways to make each short rhyme or song into a beautiful, slightly longer, piece of music that students will be proud to perform for their families and other students.

How to Make a Short Piece Longer

Form is your friend! Work with students to create a work of music from a single, simple song or rhyme. Here are some options for adding variation to a song or rhyme:

- Add hand motions to the song.
- Add body percussion (clap, pat, stomp, snap, etc.) to specific words in the song.
- Add a body percussion ostinato.
- Sing the song antiphonally, alternating lines of the song between two halves of the choir.
- Change the dynamics, tempo, or articulation.

Once you have chosen the variations that work for the particular piece, put them into an order that makes sense. Ask students to help you with this in class: "We need to make our song a little longer and more interesting for our upcoming program. Let's try some options together. You listen to hear what works best." Lead them to choose variations that fit going from one to the next. I usually aim for four to five variations and they might look something like this:

1. Students say the rhyme while keeping a beat on their laps.
2. Students say the rhyme while performing body percussion on particular, predetermined words.
3. Students say the rhyme while playing unpitched percussion instruments on the same words that had body percussion in the previous variation.
4. Students say the rhyme *in their heads* (not aloud), while playing the unpitched percussion instruments.

When you have chosen the order of your variations, suggest adding an introduction and a coda. This should be something simple, like eight beats of an ostinato pattern or even just keeping a beat patting on their laps.

When your students (and you!) are happy with the creation, think about ways to add musical expression. Can you add interest with phrasing, articulations (legato/staccato), or dynamics (softer/louder)?

What About a Recorded Program?

Many parents are not able to take time off work during the day (or even in the evening) to come to their student's performance—even though they'd love to be able to! This is particularly true in lower-income schools where people may have less flexibility with their work hours. A recorded performance could be a huge help to these families and could give your students something to work toward and to be proud of.

Should you create a video-recorded performance? Probably not. Video performances can be very difficult to complete well. They often require quite a bit of time acquiring the correct equipment, placing it correctly, and getting a good recording. But a radio show can be a great alternative.

Create a Radio Show

A radio show can be a great way to have a project that students work on that is rewarding for them, enjoyable for parents, and attainable for you. Imagine it's the 1920s and a family is gathered around the radio on Sunday afternoon listening to a melodramatic story, complete with music and sound effects. This is the kind of drama that you can build with your students in your classroom.

First, find a short script that you can do with your students. It should take at most 15 minutes from start to finish, preferably 10. I recommend searching online for "radio play for children" and try other search terms, too. Once you've found one, think about how you can add sound effects from your classroom. Aim for at least forty instances of sound effects in your 10- to 15-minute play. These can be simple dramatic effects like:

- Play a single high note on the xylophone to indicate a tense moment.
- Play the wind chimes each time a new scene begins.
- Play a glissando on a glockenspiel when something good happens.
- Play alternating fifths when characters are walking (D and A, for instance) on different sized xylophones.
- Use multiple percussion instruments to represent struggle or even a door slam.

Next, think about places you can insert songs. Aim to include three to five songs. These can be tangentially related to the action in the story. For instance, if there is a dog in the script, you might have the characters sing a song you already know about dogs.

Don't overdo the songs, just include a few throughout the script and plan a song to end with after the story concludes.

Once you've chosen sound effects and songs, type a script to use with your students that includes the instructions you want. Be sure to include a list of the spoken parts and instrument parts somewhere in your script to help you when you assign parts to your students.

Plan for at least 6 weeks of preparation for this project, using about 10--15 minutes of class time each of those weeks. Plan a dress rehearsal and a recording day (and record them both). Send a note home with students who have speaking parts asking parents to help their child read with expression and drama. Consider inviting the principal to come to one of the recording days for one of the classes.

What About Last-Minute Performance Requests?

Your principal wants you to be successful and for you to use music for the good of the whole school. What a great opportunity! This may mean, however, that your principal asks you to perform at an event with little warning or advance notice. If this happens to you, rejoice! Your principal believes in you and values what you do. Of course, it might be difficult to pull something off with such short notice. And you may feel anxious about doing it well. How do you pull off a last-minute performance?

First, say "Yes!" to the request, even if you're nervous about it. You want to build a relationship of trust with your principal. After the performance, you might mention that you'd prefer to have at least a two-week notice next time (or whatever your comfortable time-frame would be). Remember that you're serving the school community and not everyone knows what you do and how you do it.

Second, limit the number of students involved. Can you just use your choir? Can you choose one or two classes that learn quickly and that have characteristics that will make your job easier (for instance, a teacher that is happy to bring them to you at a non-traditional time or a class that has particularly clear singing voices)?

Next, choose songs and music that you've already done with the students you've selected. This is not the time to experiment with something new. Choose repertoire that is very familiar to your students and that you can lead without additional notes.

Next, limit the amount of time you will be performing and give your principal an idea of what to expect from your students. Usually, in a context like this you might think of performing for 4–10 minutes, using 2–3 pieces or songs. What and how much you do will depend on the level of the students in the program (a shorter time for younger students). Know where they will perform, for how long, and what they will do when they are done performing (Will they go back to class? Will they stay standing throughout the program? Will they sit in the audience?).

Once you know all the details, arrange your music to fit the context. Use your skills to make a short piece longer. Add simple flourishes (like a finger cymbal on each beat 4, for instance) and encourage your students to perform with smiles and to show their joy in music.

Checklist for Planning a Concert

- ☐ Ask your principal if there are specific expectations for programs at your school. You can do this by email or in person.
- ☐ For each grade that will be on the program:
  - ☐ List all the songs and musical activities you have done with them and all you plan to do before the program.
  - ☐ Note which activities and songs they particularly enjoyed.
  - ☐ Brainstorm how each of those could be presented on a program (see section "How to Make a Short Piece Longer" for how to make something small into something presentable).
- ☐ Let your principal know that you will need 20–30 minutes (and not more than that).
- ☐ Based on your time goals, decide how much time each grade will get (e.g., if only two grades will be on the program, allot 10 minutes for each). Remember to account for transition times between groups.
- ☐ Choose which selections each grade will do. Usually 2–4 selections is appropriate.
- ☐ Write up the program you planned for yourself. Include the selections each group will do and write out any comments or explanation you would like to give before or after the performances.
- ☐ Later, let your students know what they will perform and invite their input on how to present it. You will make the final choice, especially since each class in a grade may have different ideas!
- ☐ Practice their part of the program during music class for a couple weeks. You may not get to practice with everybody together.
- ☐ Check the "Checklist for a Last-Minute Performance" for details to handle the week before the performance.

Checklist for a Last-Minute Performance

- ☐ Confirm the location, date, and time with the person in charge (probably your principal).
- ☐ Check your rosters and see who is available at that time. If it is an after-school or evening performance, plan to use students who will already be at the event.
- ☐ You don't need to commit to a group of students yet. Instead, list all of the songs and musical activities that each available group has completed recently in your class.
- ☐ Decide what your objectives are for this performance: Giving students a chance to perform? Giving students a positive performing experience? Showing what they're learning? Providing a break for adults attending a meeting? Fulfilling your principal's request? Giving a flawless, beautiful interpretation of a great work of music?
- ☐ Sketch out a possible 10-minute performance that the group could do with already-known music.
- ☐ Choose some ways to make short songs, rhymes, or musical activities a little longer. See the sections "What to Include in a Program" and "How to Make a Short Piece Longer" earlier in this chapter.
- ☐ Communicate with teachers of the students you're choosing to perform. Find out if you could have any extra time with them and be sure the teachers are supportive of their students participating.
- ☐ Communicate with the person in charge of the event (probably your principal).
- ☐ Tell them that you have a *short* program that you can do—be sure to emphasize that it will be short.
- ☐ Tell them which students will participate and request additional practice time, if you think you'd like it—this could be as simple as having them show up 45 minutes early to the event.
- ☐ Ask also for any additional support you will need. For instance, you may need help moving a piano or setting up risers. Getting the help may take time, so let your principal know as early as possible what the setup will be and when you'd like it to be ready. You should not attempt to do all the setup yourself for safety reasons and for the sake of your time!
- ☐ Plan your performance. Draft how you'd like the program to go and how you will work with students to get there. Decide if you will say anything and what you will say.
- ☐ Plan your practice.
- ☐ Relax and enjoy the music and the experience with your students. Do not consider enjoyment optional—you are teaching your students the joy of performing music. Show them joy on your face and calm in your demeanor.

9

Assess What Matters

Most people I know don't remember getting grades for their music classes. There has not been a clear way of assessing what happens in the elementary music room. There are several reasons to assess your students, and I believe that, by the end of this chapter, you will find assessment can be a positive part of your day and incredibly encouraging for you and for your students. This chapter starts with why you will want to assess your students; then, what you can assess in elementary music; followed by practical steps for how to do it with many students efficiently and painlessly. Finally, I address the best times to assess.

Why Assess?

You are probably much more interested in making music with students than entering grades for them. Assessment can, however, be an asset to growing your program and building support from your school community.

Show the Progress of Your Students

The best reason for assessing your students is to show yourself and your students how much they are learning under your care—students should grow in school. Regular assessment allows you to see that they're growing and to be able to show them, their parents, and administrators that your students are learning.

Music instruction is often misunderstood by administrators, by other teachers, by parents, and even by music teachers themselves. Many people will think that you sit around the piano with children and sing songs all day long. You are one of The Wiggles, but you don't get the big bucks or the fame.

Through assessment, you can show them that music instruction is about learning music. We want our students to be able to *do* music. And we want to show people that they are learning.

Your First Year as an Elementary Music Teacher. Andrew S. Paney, Oxford University Press. © Oxford University Press 2025.
DOI: 10.1093/oso/9780197631430.003.0009

Show the Value of Your Subject

Assessment shows that music is valuable. We assess things that we care about. Students don't get a grade for lunch, for watching videos, or for attending assemblies. But they do get grades for math, writing, reading, history, science, and arts.

Assessing regularly shows that you are doing your job. It shows that you take your work seriously and that you belong in a building full of teachers and learners.

Meet Requirements

Not only is assessment a good idea, it will probably be required of you. You will need to enter grades for your students between two and six times each year. How you determine those grades is often up to you. It is better to have a plan than to throw things together at the end of a grading period. Having a plan and using it consistently will be easier for you and will help you use assessment to your benefit and to the benefit of your students.

What and How to Assess

Effort

Effort can be a difficult thing to measure in a class. It would be best to have some standards for appropriate effort in the classroom and to have ways of letting students know whether they are meeting that standard or not. For instance, you may choose to consider participation in each activity as a minimum standard. The students who do not meet that minimum standard should be told that they are not doing what is expected of them. They should have a chance to address the problem and to improve.

Singing

Singing is a main part of a music education because singing is accessible to everyone regardless of budget. It is also a form of musical expression across cultures. I see singing as a main objective for elementary music teachers because of the benefits it affords to students and because early success can mean many later benefits. Because singing is so important, it's important to have clear ways of assessing it.

With younger students, it's important to assess whether they can match appropriate pitches. Even with older students who are new to you or new to singing, an assessment for how well they are matching pitch or how well they are singing particular pitches is appropriate.

For any type of singing, having a reasonable evaluation scale that can be used consistently and that will mean the same thing to you today as it does in six weeks is important. For example, you might use a 3-point scale with 1 meaning does not meet standard, 2 meaning is approaching the standard, and 3 meaning meets the standard. For a simple rubric like this, the evaluation question needs to be very specific. A question like, "Sings at grade level," is not specific enough and does not give enough information to evaluate growth. instead, a prompt like "Can echo a so mi pattern successfully" will give more information.

Instrument Playing

When evaluating students on playing an instrument, it is best to have a clear set of expectations and a clear set of standards for the students. Some basic items to assess are how a student holds the instrument or the mallets, how the student produces a sound on the instruments, whether the sound is the appropriate sound, whether the student controls the instrument when he or she is not playing it, and whether a student shows proper care for an instrument.

Music Reading and Writing

This is an area of assessment that can lead to an interest in learning and an increase in self-efficacy for students. When your assessment objectives are clear and carefully sequenced, you can make them known to students and encourage them to grow in particular areas, to keep practicing, and sometimes just to wait for their brains to develop. You may even find that your students especially enjoy assessment. When there are clear goals, learning can become like a game for students. They want to improve and they want to reach the next level. This is the principle on which video games are designed and which makes students love video games: there's a level of difficulty but the judging is fair. Even though they can't do something in a video game, they know that if they keep trying they will be able to do it and the rules won't change.

For assessing music reading, at the most basic level, pitch reading can involve following a line that goes up and down and matching the direction with a neutral syllable like la. The assessment item could be something like "student can follow melodic contour from the whiteboard with their voice" and the input from you could be a simple yes or no. Or, if you prefer, a number rating system. The next section includes a model of a rubric for each item and includes both options.

How to Use Verbal and Aural Assessments

Verbal and aural assessments include anything where the response from students is spoken, sung, or played. Though these are not as easily recorded and not nearly as objective nor as easy to understand as written assignments, especially for other adults, they're incredibly important for a subject like music, where what we do is aural.

Often these kinds of assessments will be informal and will involve you asking a question and students responding either by yelling out answers or by raising their hand in responding. These kinds of assessments can help you know how far along your class is and how much more practice you need to do on a particular concept. If you choose to include this kind of assessment in your grading, you will need to have a way to record or write down what students say or how they perform in the verbal assessment.

Perhaps the best way to record students' responses is by using a rubric. A rubric not only adds credibility to your evaluation but also is faster and a lot easier to complete with students. An added bonus is that administrators and other teachers understand rubrics. A third benefit is that it allows you to see students' improvement over time as you use the evaluation again.

A good rubric is simple to use and clear on what it is measuring. I recommend using a standard, 3- or 5-point rubric that evaluates students' competence on particular skills. If you look at articles on rubrics online you'll see that many articles have very specific rubrics with several explanations for each number of the rubric. This can be a smart idea when judges are from various backgrounds and you want scores to reflect the same things for each judge. But these kinds of rubrics take a long time to learn and can be complicated in the moment. Perhaps the most complicated part of them is that often students' responses don't fit clearly into one of the descriptors. Instead, I recommend a simple rubric with the option of using a yes/no or number rating system. Here's an example:

Rubric for Aural Assessment

Student can read a 4-beat motive *ta* and *tadi* from a flash card.

Achieved standard? Yes No

Teacher rating: 1 2 3 4 5

How to Use Written Assessments

Written work is by far the easiest to use for assessment. It is the most common in educational settings and the easiest to use in an objective way. The difficult part of written assessment is finding a way to measure the thing that you want to measure. I recommend finding some worksheets, quizzes, or tests that others have made online or from friends. Later, after you've seen the work of others in this area, you may want to make some adjustments and create something that perfectly fits your needs.

I recommend not using standard music worksheets online but instead finding ones that meet your objectives for each grade and that fit the things that they already know. Instead of teaching new material, worksheets should be helping students practice material that they already know, to build speed and gain fluency in those skills.

Written work can present challenges for some learners. Keeping this in mind will help you to do what is best for each of your students. Creating some modifications for certain assignments is not usually a difficult task and it's one that students' teachers will be able to help you with thinking about and designing. You will receive information about special learners in your class at the beginning of the year. If you don't receive any, you should expect that something went wrong and that they are still coming. Ask at the office for I.E.P. (individualized education plan) data for all the students that come to see you. You have a right to see this information and you need to see it to serve your students as well as possible. If you suspect a student may have different learning needs but you haven't received any information about that student, the easiest way to proceed is to ask the classroom teacher if any students need modifications with assignments. The classroom teacher will know these things offhand and will be able to help you quickly. You don't need to mention specific students' names unless they ask.

Written Assessment Styles

The easiest written work to evaluate is multiple choice questions. You can use a key, and grading is very quick. Fill-in-the-blank questions are a close second. As you design your assessments, be sure to consider how many students will take the assessment and how you plan to grade it. The best assessment that takes too long to evaluate will not do you much good.

One of the best results of using written work in the music classroom is that it is understandable to administrators, other teachers, and parents. They know that you are doing something and you have evidence of it on paper.

Written assignments in music can be an effective and objective measure of students' learning. For younger students, this can be very simple worksheets with just two or three responses. For older students this can be fill-in-the-blank worksheets and creative assignments that the students enjoy completing.

As with any assignment, it is important that written assignments match your objectives for the course. Busy work is not a benefit to students, but practice in musical skills is! As you are planning for each grade level's objectives, keep in mind the kinds of written assessments that might match your objectives. You can find these online, you can create them yourself, or you can often find good examples in textbooks the school already owns.

Another big benefit of written assignments is that other people can administer them. I like to create large packets that students can complete with a substitute teacher when I'm absent. I create these assignments using worksheets that I've found online—crossword puzzles and word searches that reinforce musical vocabulary we've already covered and that allow students to apply musical concepts. I make these packets quite large, usually four pages front and back, so that no student will finish the packet in the class period—I don't want idle students!

Written assessments can evaluate students' knowledge of music vocabulary and even their aural skills. One example of a written assignment that younger students can do is a modified dictation assignment. A simple rhythmic dictation, like the one below, can be enjoyable for students and easy for you to administer and evaluate.

Rhythm Dictation Example

Either by computer or by hand, create a quiz that is five questions long. Each question will include just two rhythms. You will instruct students to circle the one that you perform. It might look like this (Figure 9.1):

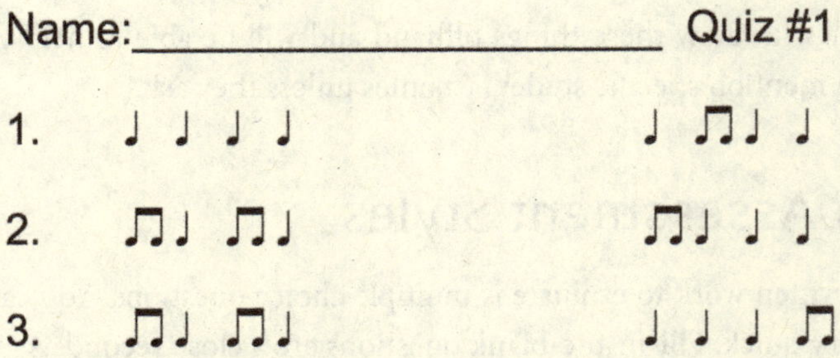

Name:____________________ Quiz #1

1. ♩ ♩ ♩ ♩ ♩ ♫ ♩ ♩

2. ♫ ♩ ♫ ♩ ♫ ♩ ♩ ♩

3. ♫ ♩ ♫ ♩ ♩ ♩ ♩ ♫

FIGURE 9.1 A model of a simple dictation quiz.

After passing out the quizzes, say, "Listen and circle the rhythm I perform. Number one." Then clap a rhythm and waits for the students to respond. The first time you do an assessment like this, you may want to do an example together on the board. You'll find that younger (and older) students find this activity to be like a game.

Pre- and Posttest Assessments

As in any school subject, our main objective is that students learn! The easiest and most clear way to show learning is by evaluating a skill and then evaluating it again several weeks later. How you design an assessment is important, but like most things, you can learn as you go, and make improvements each year. There are some things to remember as you prepare an assessment that will measure progress. For instance, you don't want students to be anxious or distressed that they don't perform well on the pretest. You can do this by telling them that you are going to give them the same test now and at the end of the semester. You can also do this by making it a written exam where they don't necessarily know if they're doing it correctly at the time. Another option on a written pre- and posttest assessment is to include an option that is "I don't know." One thing you don't want is for students not to respond to items on the assessment. Younger students don't often care about grades, but we still want to design these things so that they feel like an enjoyable activity rather than a serious test.

You may choose to do this kind of assessment for yourself, rather than for a grade for students. This will let you know how you are doing and in what ways you still need to review information. you can even tell this to your older students. They would love to know that you are being evaluated, too.

For students' benefit, especially older students, it is great to be able to show them how far they have come and how much they have improved. Growth is something that you can celebrate with each student and with the whole class. You can even conduct some pre- and posttest assessments for the entire class and allow them to see their improvement as a group. You could chart their progress on items like "Percentage of students singing at pitch," or, "Amount of time it takes to line up quietly at the door." These assessments can help student develop a sense of class ownership and pride.

When to Assess

Not Only at the End!

Assessment can be a joy for you and for your students. Plan to assess multiple times throughout the year and make both less formal and more formal assessments. When you play an echo game, take some quick notes. Just a check, plus, or minus will benefit your planning and can give you a record of your students' growth.

Will you have a final exam in your class? Probably not. Instead, think of small ways to assess the things that really matter and assess them regularly at least every few weeks.

It may help to ask other teachers in your building how they evaluate their students and what report cards look like. Many elementary schools do not give letter grades for young students, but give parents a sheet of students' progress on particular things, for example, how many letters a student can identify, whether a student can add numbers up to 5, or whether a student can answer simple questions about a short story. As mentioned in Chapter 4, following regular protocols from your school can be a benefit to you, to your students, and to others in the building. Assessing your students in the way the other teachers in your school assess them will help the classroom teachers understand your evaluations, your principal understand what you do, and parents to have a consistent experience throughout the building. Unfortunately, this is not usually set out for you in an easy way. You will have to do the work to figure out what other teachers are doing and to modify it to your particular instruction. This kind of task is worth it! It will eventually make grading much easier for you and it will show others the value of your subject.

Routines and Assessment

One way to make assessment painless is to make it regular. Once it becomes part of your routine, it will become easier for you, more useful for you, and even something students expect, are comfortable with, and enjoy. Plan assessment into your lesson plans. Aim to assess on something, however small, at least once a week. Once you know what you want to assess, work on adding that into your regular classroom routine.

One way to do this is to use codes within your seating charts. In Chapter 3, I suggested creating seating charts with eight little squares for you to add information about students. Don't be stingy in filling in those squares! Include the information you want and include a key so that you know what each square is for. When you run out of squares, simply print another seating chart for that class.

Another way to do this is with flashcards. Some teachers have had great success with putting each child's name on its own flash card, in addition to using their seating chart. When they are assessing students in class, they simply take out their flashcards and call on the student in the front of the card stack. They then note the student's performance on that task. If it takes more than one class period to complete an assessment, they just put the students who still need to complete the assessment at the front of the pack of cards. When grades are due, they alphabetize the cards and enter their notes or evaluations into the school's grading system.

Checklist for Assessing What Matters

- ☐ Ask your principal or supervisor if a particular assessment is required for your classes. If so, follow it! If not, create your own.
- ☐ List the areas you want to assess with your students. I suggest singing, written work, effort, instrument playing, and music reading and writing.
- ☐ List the skills you want your students to be able to do in each of the areas above.
- ☐ List the knowledge you want them to know.
- ☐ Decide whether to assess with an observation rubric or with written work (a quiz, test, or worksheet).
  - Create the quiz, test, or worksheet.
  - Create a rubric for each of the areas you will assess.
- ☐ Choose just three skills to assess this first year. You can choose different skills or knowledge for each grade level, but keep it simple.
- ☐ Decide if you can put your assessments onto your seating chart for ease of use.
- ☐ Decide when to complete your assessments and schedule them so you won't leave it to the end of the term.

10

Survive a Hard Day

Introduction

Every job has challenges. How you respond to them affects the outcome. In this chapter I hope to help you build resilience and avoid pitfalls.

You will have difficult days, probably several of them. Expect that you will, and have a plan for how you will handle it. I recommend the following:

Expect a hard day.
Tell somebody about the hard day.
Choose an outlet for what you are feeling.
Keep going.

This chapter will take you through those steps.

Expect a Hard Day

You care about doing a good job, that's why you've read this far in the book! But things won't always turn out the way you plan. Some extremely well-planned lessons fall flat. Sometimes you make mistakes that you really wish you hadn't made. How will you respond when it happens to you?

The first day I was teaching a new fifth grade music class, I prepared extremely well. I knew exactly what needed to happen and had memorized and practiced my plan. The room I was teaching in was quite small and I needed to play the piano, use the back of the piano to hang a visual aid, and, later in the lesson, move the piano so students could see the board that I had prepared with the next task. It was important to me to keep the lesson moving at a quick pace, both to avoid discipline problems that day, and also to set the tone for music classes for the rest of the year.

Your First Year as an Elementary Music Teacher. Andrew S. Paney, Oxford University Press. © Oxford University Press 2025.
DOI: 10.1093/oso/9780197631430.003.0010

My lesson was progressing well and I was keeping the pace I had planned for. When it was time to move the piano, I started to push it out of the way quickly, to keep the flow of my lesson. Instead of a smooth transition, CRASH! The piano fell over onto its back and was lying flat on the floor, covering up my visual and making an astounding sound. Teachers in other parts of the building, even upstairs, came to see what had happened. It turns out the wheels on the piano locked up when I pushed it and, instead of rolling, the piano tilted on the axis of those locked rear wheels. The rest of the day I taught with the piano laying on the floor. I couldn't use the piano for my lessons and I couldn't use the visual aid it was covering up. At the end of the day, four maintenance workers had to lift the piano up.

Here are some other examples of incidents that made for a tough day for teachers I talked to while writing this book:

Two girls start fighting at the very beginning of class and have to be removed by staff.

You left your computer at home and all of your lessons and audio and visual examples were on it.

Your stomach starts to hurt, but you don't want to miss teaching.

You have a fire drill just as you're about to start the best part of your lesson.

A student accuses you of treating them unfairly.

The noise in the cafeteria while you're on lunch duty gives you a headache.

Your car gets vandalized (or a flat tire or won't start).

You realize there is an embarrassing stain on your clothes in the middle of your fourth class.

You get bad news about a friend or family member while you're teaching.

You spill your coffee (or someone else does) before you've even tasted it.

You forget your lunch and have no time to get any more food.

When you experience a day like that, where things don't go as planned, it's important to keep a proper perspective and to know what you will do. One thing that helped me the day the piano fell was remembering how many teachers had told me that the first year was the hardest. I allowed myself to make mistakes in the first year, expecting that things would get easier the next year. And they did!

Take Care of Yourself

Plan now, while you're feeling good, for how you will care for yourself. You are the one who can help your body, mind, and emotions grow and become more resilient. This means getting the right amount of sleep, eating well, getting regular and vigorous exercise, spending time outside, and planning for fun, non-work times in your week.[1]

Tell Somebody

Most teachers are extremely sympathetic and know that teaching is a hard job. They will be supportive when you come to them with problems or just to share discouragement or even feelings of inadequacy. Teachers have had those same experiences and feelings. Don't be afraid to share with another teacher (it doesn't need to be a music teacher). You might start a discussion with someone with, "Can I share something that bothered me today?" Or just ask, "How is your day going?" and expect that they will return the question (you can also, of course, just tell them even if they don't ask).

Another time, my principal was upset with me for something (I can't remember what). She was very upset and I didn't know what to do about it. I told my supervisor, another music teacher at another building, about it and told her that I didn't know what to do. This music teacher said, in an offhand, unconcerned way, "She'll get over it." It wasn't what I expected or wanted to hear, but it was good advice. Instead of worrying about the problem, I focused on doing my work and showing kindness to my principal. The issue never came up again and the principal and I had a positive relationship—so much so that I don't remember what the issue was to begin with!

A friend or family member can offer the support you need, too. Just find someone positive who will encourage you to keep going and to listen to all you have to say.

Notice What You're Feeling

What are you feeling? What do you expect you will feel on a tough day? Will you be frustrated? Sad? Angry? Disappointed? Exhausted? Tough days can wear you out and make you rethink your career choice. Plan to make this explicit by saying it aloud to yourself or writing it down: "I'm feeling frustrated right now," or "I'm feeling angry right now because my principal said something that upset me."

Choose an Outlet

This happens to everyone in almost every career. Don't give up. As soon as possible, choose an energizing or relaxing activity to calm your mind and your body. Remember, everyone has bad days.

You need a way to tame your mind. Vigorous exercise is a great way to do it.

Keep Going

Don't stop. It gets better. No problem is unsolvable. You can get over it and can learn to do it better.

Flowchart for a Tough Day

Instead of a checklist, here is a flowchart for what to do when you have a tough day. Sometimes it can be difficult to make any decision after a day because you are mentally and physically exhausted. Instead, just go through the list below and complete each item in order.

1. Acknowledge that it was a tough day. Say out loud, "This was a tough day."
2. Talk to someone as soon as possible. Call a friend or stop by a trusted person's house and say, "I had a tough day, can I tell you about it?"
3. Tell your friend what you're going to do to engage your mind and your body in something different: "I'm going to the gym (or coffee shop, a friend's house, etc.)."
4. Do it! Get some vigorous exercise or dive into a novel or just take a walk outside.
5. Commit to keep going. Say out loud to yourself: "I can do this. I am a trained musician and a trained teacher. I will find a way to the other side of this problem."

11

Become a Better Teacher

Challenge and Reward

If you want a long, satisfying career in music education, you will need to plan for how you will get better at what you do. You will probably have to do professional development to keep your certification, but how you do it is often up to you. Do you want to check the boxes as quickly and easily as possible? You certainly can do that! Or do you want to use the time to build your skills and create a beautiful oasis of music in the lives of your students and colleagues? This might rest fully on your taking initiative to make it happen—it's likely no one will be telling you that you must take a course or improve your skills in a particular way.

There is an intrinsic reward for challenging yourself and persisting through difficult circumstances. You will know that you have accomplished something important and that you have improved some aspect of your teaching. The two ways I want to challenge you to work on becoming a better teacher are (1) building your team and (2) building your skills.

Build a Team

Teaching elementary music can be a lonely job. It is likely that no one else in your building will do exactly what you do. Who are your peers? Who can you count on to notice when you're not there or not feeling your best? This is up to you! It's great to connect with teachers at your building who you will see every day. You also need to have some other music teacher friends who can understand more specific aspects of your challenges. These can be other teachers nearby or far away. Look back to Chapter 2, "Meet Your Team," for ideas on how to create this essential part of having a successful, satisfying career as a music teacher.

Your First Year as an Elementary Music Teacher. Andrew S. Paney, Oxford University Press. © Oxford University Press 2025.
DOI: 10.1093/oso/9780197631430.003.0011

Outside of your particular school, you will need friends and mentors who are elementary music teachers. A great way to meet these people is to go to music teacher workshops put on by music education organizations. You can find these people by searching on social media and by attending online and in-person events. As a bonus, these events will often count toward your professional development requirements. If you're in a place with a lot of options, I recommend choosing one (or at most two) organizations and really digging in there—attend everything and make it a priority to know the people there. This deep commitment is how you plant the roots of meaningful friendships and start to enjoy your professional community.

Build Skills

Building your teaching skills will impact hundreds (or thousands) of people around you: your students, your team, and yourself. Keep this in mind when you are making financial and time sacrifices to improve your teaching.

One of the best ways to improve your teaching, to make your life richer, and to make your teaching more enjoyable is to take a summer class. There are several options for you that will give you a certificate in a particular focus of teaching: Orff, Kodály, and more. All of these will help you grow as a musician and as a teacher. Visit the organization websites and check their social media pages for information about how to get started. Here are the names, acronyms, and websites of the larger approaches in the United States:

American Eurhythmics Society (AES), americaneurhythmics.org.
American Orff Schulwerk Association (AOSA), aosa.org.
Dalcroze Society of America (DSA), dalcrozeusa.org.
Feierabend Association for Music Education (FAME), feierabendmusic.org.
Music Will, musicwill.org.
Organization of American Kodály Educators (OAKE), oake.org.
Songworks Educators Association (SWEA), songworkseducatorsassociation.com.
The Gordon Institute for Music Learning (GIML), giml.org.
World Music Drumming (WMD), worldmusicdrumming.com.
World Music Pedagogy (WMP), worldmusicpedagogy.com.

How do you choose? You will have to do some research to find where courses are offered. It might be best to choose something that is active locally where you're teaching, if you're looking to build your team. For each of these, you should expect a 2- to 3-week commitment over the summer. You will work hard and spend perhaps the entire day working hard to build skills. In this hard work you will also build connections to others with similar values and goals of improving their music teaching. You will make lifelong friendships at these intense training sessions and have great opportunities to serve other music teachers and to benefit from the experiences of other music teachers.

Checklist for Becoming a Better Music Teacher

Build a Team

- ☐ List four teachers you know that you can count on. These can be young teachers who were studying with you in university or experienced teachers you know through church, community groups, or even through student teaching.
- ☐ List the names of two or three teachers who work in your building, people you think you can trust and go to with problems.
- ☐ Look up music education organizations near you and put their upcoming events on your calendar. When you go, plan to be kind, smile, initiate conversations, arrive early, and stay late.

Build Skills

- ☐ Visit music education organization websites and list the chapters that are near you for those listed in this chapter and any others you have heard about.
- ☐ Ask music teachers you know for their thoughts on pursuing certification in Orff, Kodály, Gordon, or another approach.
- ☐ Choose whichever one you think you might most enjoy and commit to pursuing it. I recommend sticking with one approach through all the training, rather than sampling a little of each.

PART III

Musical Activities

12

Activities for Beginning and Ending Class

Introduction

Beginnings and endings are important. This chapter details steps for starting and ending each class session with order and joy.

The Importance of Routines

Children generally work very well with routines. The entire school day is full of routines, and teaching them makes everything easier for students and for teachers. Since you will probably see your students just once or a few times each week, having a clear procedure for how things will happen in your classroom will be a huge benefit to you (and to your students). You will have fewer discipline issues and be able to save your voice for instruction of music, rather than for telling students what will happen next or what they're supposed to be doing.

Should You Call Roll?

Many schools will require you to have a record of attendance. I've seen teachers call the roll at the beginning of the class period, just saying each child's name and waiting for them to respond with "Here" or "Present." This is an extremely inefficient way of accomplishing that task and has no musical value. There are two better ways to find out who is present and who is absent: (1) Use a musical game or (2) Use your seating chart.

The easiest way to take attendance quickly is to simply look at your seating chart and where your students are sitting (if they're sitting on chairs) and note the absent students. I usually ask the class about missing students: "I see that Paul and Georgine are absent

Your First Year as an Elementary Music Teacher. Andrew S. Paney, Oxford University Press. © Oxford University Press 2025.
DOI: 10.1093/oso/9780197631430.003.0012

today. Is that correct?" This allows students to confirm that they are in fact absent, tell me that they are running late, or even point out another student that I may have missed that is also missing. This process takes about 15 seconds total.

Another efficient and effective way to take roll is to create a game or musical procedure for taking roll. You, the teacher, start a beat with clapping and/or patting and call out students' names over a set number of beats. For instance, you might start a 4-beat ostinato, pat-clap-pat-clap, and say a student's name on the first two beats and invite them to respond with "I'm here" on the second two beats. You call the roll in order, but each child gets to respond alone, getting some personal attention from you (and eye contact!) and from the others in the class, too.

This musical call-and-response can be developed throughout the school year and made slightly more interesting and fun for you and your students. You can give them some multiple-choice options for how they respond:

> "I'm here" on quarter notes,
> "I'm present" with quarter note and two eighth notes,
> "I-am-sit-ting in-my chair" on sixteenth notes, eighth notes, and a quarter note, etc.

Of course, you won't mention the note lengths in this exercise, just allow them to *do* them. Later you can add a limited number of pitches, too. You sing on one or two pitches and students sing back on the same pitches.

The main value of the first option above is efficiency and giving you lots of class time. The main value of the second option is creating a musical routine that allows each student to have individual attention and eventually allows for some musical choices and even improvisation.

Beginning Class with Younger Students

Routines are particularly important with younger students. Since so many things are new for them in the world, many of them thrive on knowing what will happen next and what their role is. They will delight in starting class in the same way each day. My main objective in the first 5–10 minutes of class with younger students is to make happy music together. This means we sing songs that involve everyone singing the same thing, we do musical games together, we smile, we sing familiar songs, and we learn simple, new songs and rhymes that bring smiles to their faces.

Many teachers will begin with a greeting like, "Hello, children" sung on *so* and *mi* (s m s m). Students respond with "Hello, Mr. Paney" sung on the same pitches (ss mm s m). This can be a great kickoff to calling a musical roll as describe above. This is a fine way to start the class, give it a try! Note that it will not be successful the first few times—you will need to train them for your beginning class routine! Also, note that this is *not* recommended for older students (first or second grade is the oldest I'd recommend for this, unless you've developed the habit and they expect it from previous year with you as their teacher).

I preferred to start my class with body percussion each time. As soon as class began, I would clap a 4-beat rhythm pattern and my students would echo. I would follow this immediately with reading of rhythm flashcards. Some days we'd read fifteen or twenty cards, other days we'd just read four or five. It was important to keep the pattern, the recurring procedure, for my students so that we could start the class period well. It gave them some transition time and the comfort of knowing exactly what they could expect to do when they came into the room. I did vary the cards we used or something about the reading (for instance, read it in a strong voice, a monster voice, a sheep voice, etc.).

Beginning Class with Older Students

Routines can help with older students, too, but you'll need to work a little harder to avoid tedium. I recommend starting with body percussion and rhythm reading, just like you do with younger students. But add a little variation as the weeks progress. For instance, you could speed up the tempo a little bit or have them clap the rhythms they read instead of saying them. See Part IV of this book for more ideas to use with flashcards.

To be clear, the body percussion and rhythm cards should be the very first thing students do, even before taking roll or any announcements. I think it's best to start with the music before even greeting the class! Especially with students who are new to you, it's good to have a nonverbal way to say that it's time to start class. Once you finish the first activity, you can immediately start the next activity or give your announcement or take roll. I like the body percussion because you don't have to say (and repeat), "Quiet down, please," or "It's time to start now, eyes up here." You just start with a pattern and they repeat it.

Ending Class

With younger students it is especially important to have a routine for ending music class. For first grade and younger, I use a song as my closing song. I always, *always*, end class with the same short song. This familiarity makes it easier for the students to transition out of music time and into the next thing. Some young students will be extremely disappointed when music class ends. Singing the final song can ease them into the next part of their day. There are several options and I recommend you choose one that you like, since you'll be singing it many, many times. I use "Firefly," a Japanese melody with an English adaptation.[1] I love the simple, beautiful melody and students enjoy it, too.

With older students, the end of class is not as significant. They do fine with transitions between classes. My recommendation is to have them help you reset the room by making sure all chairs are in the right place, putting away any instruments or other materials, erasing the board, and setting the room up nicely for your next class. Involve them in the process and let them know what grade is coming next. They may be very interested in helping set up the room the way you need it, whether it's for another class from the same grade or for a different grade.

Once the room is ready, have them line up at the door and play a game with them or even just chat for a bit. Ask them what they are doing next, where their favorite restaurants are, what music they like to listen to, etc. Any games that can work in a standing line that aren't too exciting are good choices, too. I don't recommend doing rhythm flashcards again, since that's a part of the beginning class routine. Instead, choose something that it easy to stop abruptly and that keeps students interested, but doesn't increase their excitement level too high.

Some In-Line Games

Once your students are lined up, you may need to guide them in some activities to keep them calm and ready for their next class. This is also a great time to practice some things you want them to know or do. It's best to keep this incredibly fun and a joy for your students. You can make it a joyful, positive end to their music time. Here are some games that can work with older and younger students.

Guess the song. You hum a melody and they guess what it is by raising their hands. This is a good opportunity to review a new song you just taught and also to remind your students of something you haven't done in a while. I recommend keeping it to songs you do in class, since you don't know what music they listen to outside of your class. This keeps the playing field level for all students and doesn't make some think that they aren't in the same culture as others.

I spy with my little eye. You choose some item in the room and say, "I spy with my little eye something blue." Students raise their hands to ask a question about what you see. Play continues until someone correctly identifies the blue item you chose. With some classes you can have a student do the next round. With the youngest students I recommend that you be the leader each time. Then you can move quickly into the next game after someone guesses it.

Twenty Questions. Think of an object, any object, but perhaps one you've talked about in class. Ask students to quietly raise their hands to ask questions to guess what the object is. All questions must have "yes" or "no" answers. Play continues until they guess it. For more fun, keep track of how many guesses it takes them to guess and challenge them to beat their record.

Sing a Song. If you don't want to do a game, you can just sing a song for them, even one you haven't done in class. Story songs or ballads are great for this time. You can even stop one mid-story if their teacher arrives before you finish. They will make you promise to sing the rest at the next music class.

13

Games to Get Older Students *Doing* Music in the First Weeks

Introduction

Building rapport is most important with older students. These games help with that objective. All of these can be used in the first weeks of class, but they require minimal music knowledge.

The games in this chapter have a record of success with upper elementary students (ages 9 and up). Playing music games will build your older students' musical skills and help you gain rapport with them. Of course you can play these games with younger students, but I prefer to save these for when they're older, since younger students enjoy many more types of activities.

Keep in mind that these are *practice* activities. Your students need to know things before they play them! I suggest using Rhythm Lesson #1 on the first day of class and then using a game on the second day. All of the games in this chapter can be played with just the two rhythms they learn in Rhythm Lesson #1. As your students learn new rhythms and other musical elements, incorporate them into the game to add difficulty and to give students practice opportunities.

You will notice these are all rhythm games. There are some great games for practicing melody in the next chapter, but you probably won't play those in your first few weeks of class. Learning rhythms is so important to developing musicianship, and I recommend focusing only on rhythms for the first few weeks. This is the best way to get students *doing* music as early as possible.

All games presented here can be played by students with varying abilities. Students with limited mobility can play these games successfully and fully, since none require moving around the room. I've used these games with students with visual and auditory needs successfully with minimal accommodations. Though there is competition in these games, there are enough opportunities to practice and to recover from mistakes that no

Your First Year as an Elementary Music Teacher. Andrew S. Paney, Oxford University Press. © Oxford University Press 2025.
DOI: 10.1093/oso/9780197631430.003.0013

student feels humiliated for participating. As the teacher, you can help students develop an atmosphere of respect and mutual encouragement. Model using encouraging words and normalize mistakes!

Using Rhythm Syllables

I do not recommend using official names ("quarter note," "eighth note") this early in the process. They're not necessary for completing these lessons and can be more confusing than helpful. Students will learn those names later in the year. Instead, have them say rhythm syllables as they read rhythms.

Which rhythm syllables should you use? It matters very much *that* you use a system. It does not matter, however, *which* system you use. I recommend using a system that gives a name to each rhythm and does *not* keep track of which beat they are on. Choose exactly one system (don't mix them) and use it every time. For this book I will use the first recommended system below, the Takadimi system. Feel free to adjust activities and lessons to a different system, if you'd like to.

Rhythm Reading Systems

Choose *one* system from those on the left and use it every time with your students. The names of the systems on the left, for your reference, are the Takadimi, Gordon, and Galin-Paris-Chevé counting systems.

How should beginners read this rhythm?

Recommended for Beginners	Not Recommended for Beginners
"Ta tadi takadimi ta"	"One two-and three-e-and-a four"
"du du-de du-ta-de-ta du."	"One two-tay three-ta-tay-ta four"
"ta titi tikitiki ta"	

Rhythm Lesson #1

You can teach this brief lesson on the first day of class. It will give your older students something musical they can do right away: distinguish between one and two sounds on a beat.

Objective

- Students will label and distinguish between one and two sounds on a beat.

Materials

- Marker board and marker.

Rhythm flash cards with only ♩ (quarter notes) and ♫ (pairs of eighth notes) patterns, included in ▶Visual 16.5 in Appendix A.

Step by Step

1. Say, "Echo me," and clap 4-beat patterns that include only ♩ and ♫. For example, you might clap ♩ ♩ ♩ ♩, ♩ ♩ ♩ ♫, ♩ ♩ ♫ ♩, or ♩ ♩ ♫ ♫. Students echo each 4-beat pattern you clap.
2. After completing several (7–10) patterns, clap this pattern: ♩ ♩ ♫ ♩
3. Repeat the same pattern after they echo.
4. Without clapping it again, say "Clap that pattern again, please."
5. After they clap, ask, "Which of these do you think represents that pattern?" Show them the following patterns on the board, either handwritten or on flash cards: ♩ ♩ ♩ ♩ and ♩ ♩ ♫ ♩. When they answer, ask them why they chose that one.
6. Point to the quarter note and say, "That's right! In music, this symbol stands for one sound on a beat and we call it '*ta*.' Can you find any other *tas*?"
7. Point to the pair of eighth notes and say, "This other symbol stands for two sounds on one beat and we call it '*tadi*.' You would read this pattern '*ta ta tadi ta*.' Read it for me." Students read it aloud.
8. Try other patterns, too. "How would you read this one?" ♩ ♩ ♫ ♫ "What about this?" ♩ ♩ ♩ ♫ Students read other patterns. Continue to give different 4-beat patterns that use exclusively those two rhythms (♩ and ♫) while students read them.
9. Have students read several flashcards that use only *ta* and *tadi*, see "Flashcards 1: Just Read" game.

Fun with Flash Cards

Flashcard activities require very little preparation or setup, children enjoy them, and they allow students to practice quite a lot of material quickly. There is just enough challenge in these activities to keep students interested. Remember that these activities should be used with rhythms students know, not new rhythms. On the first day of class, after completing Rhythm Lesson #1, do any of the following activities, but use cards that have only *tas* and *tadi*s on them. Later, do the same activities again as students learn each new rhythm.

I recommend starting with the first activity and progressing through the list adding just one new activity each week. Don't be afraid to repeat an activity at the next class period—familiarity can be good! I've included more flashcard games in the next chapter (that you probably won't get to in the first 3 weeks) for when your students are ready for a new challenge. Note that I wrote these instructions for 4-beat flashcards, but these activities will work well with flashcards in almost any meter.

Objective

- Practice reading known rhythms.

Materials

- Appropriate flashcards (see ▶Visual 16.5 in Appendix A for printable flashcards).

Setup

- Face the students and hold the cards so that all students can see them.

How to Play

Flashcards 1: Just Read

1. Hold selected flashcards where all students can see them.
2. Count them in aloud, "one, two, three, four" and point to each beat as they read it aloud, using rhythm syllables.
3. If they read it correctly, move immediately to the next card without missing a beat, counting again before they read.

Extension: As their reading improves, avoid pointing to the beats as they read. Instead, ask them to keep a beat while they read. I recommend having them keep a beat by patting their laps with both hands (for younger students) or with just one hand (for older students). Clapping can be too loud for students to be able to hear the rhythms they are saying.

Flashcards 2: Flash Memory

This is identical to Flashcards 1, but you only allow them to see the card while you're counting, not while they are reading. Use a table or a music stand so that you can flip the card down while they're reading. It's OK if they see the next card in the stack as you flip the card down.

1. Show students a card while you count them in, "one, two, three, four." Flip the card down when you say "four" so that they can't see it and must read from memory.
2. Students read the card they can no longer see.
3. If they read it correctly, move on to the next card immediately, without missing a beat.
4. If they make a mistake, show them the card again and let them try it again. If they make many mistakes, they probably are not ready for this activity, move back to Flashcards 1: Just Read.

Flashcards 3: Selective Reading

This is identical to Flashcards 1, but students read just one rhythm when it occurs. This provides a bit of a challenge and helps them listen to each other and develop their skills in making music together.

1. Divide the students into two (or more) groups and assign each group a rhythm. For example, "If you're wearing glasses, read only the *tas*, if you're not, read only the *tadis*."
2. Students read just their assigned rhythm on each card.
3. Repeat with several cards (8–10).
4. If they are doing well, reassign the parts so that students are reading a different rhythm.

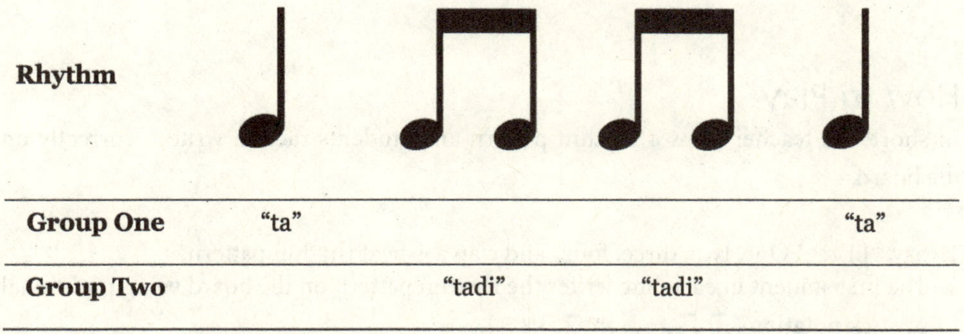

FIGURE 13.1 Example of game "Flashcards 3: Selective Reading." In this activity, a class of students is divided into two groups and each reads only their assigned rhythm.

Rhythm Race

Students love this fast-paced, exciting game. It allows you to practice many rhythms while students are motivated by the friendly, low-stakes competition.

Objectives

- Review known rhythms.
- Nonmusical: Build class identity.
- Nonmusical: Build excitement and expend some energy.

Materials

- Marker board or chalkboard.
- 2–5 dry erase markers or chalk pieces, one for each team.
- Optional: Appropriate rhythm cards (ones that include only rhythms students have learned).

Setup

- Group size: 6–30 students (ages 9 and up).
- 2–5 lines of students facing the board, 3–6 students in each line.

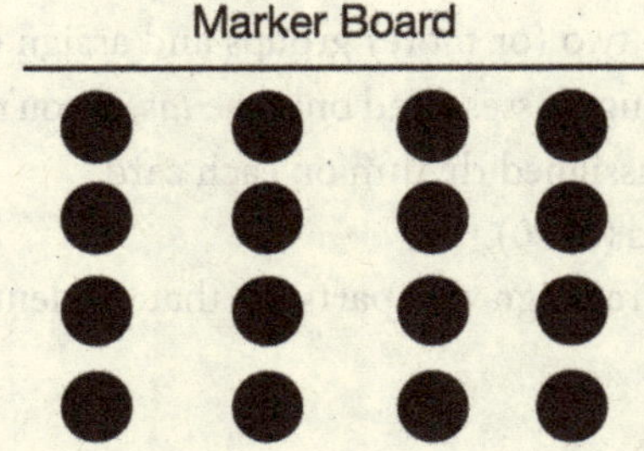

FIGURE 13.2 Arrangement of lines of students for Rhythm Race.

How to Play

In short, the teacher claps a rhythm pattern and students race to write it correctly on the board.

1. Say, "Listen! One, two, three, four," and clap a 4-beat rhythm pattern.
2. The first student in each line writes the rhythm pattern on the board using traditional or stick notation (♫♫♩ ♩ or ⊓⊓| |.)
3. When the student is satisfied with their answer, they "pop down" below their written answer by squatting quickly. Once they pop down, their answer is sealed and cannot be changed. The round concludes when all people at the board have popped down.
4. Assign scores: Each correct answer gets one point. One additional point is earned for popping down first with the correct answer.
5. Students write their score as a tally by their team name at the top of their work area, then give the marker or chalk to the next person in line and walk to the end of their line.
6. Repeat the steps with the next students in line.

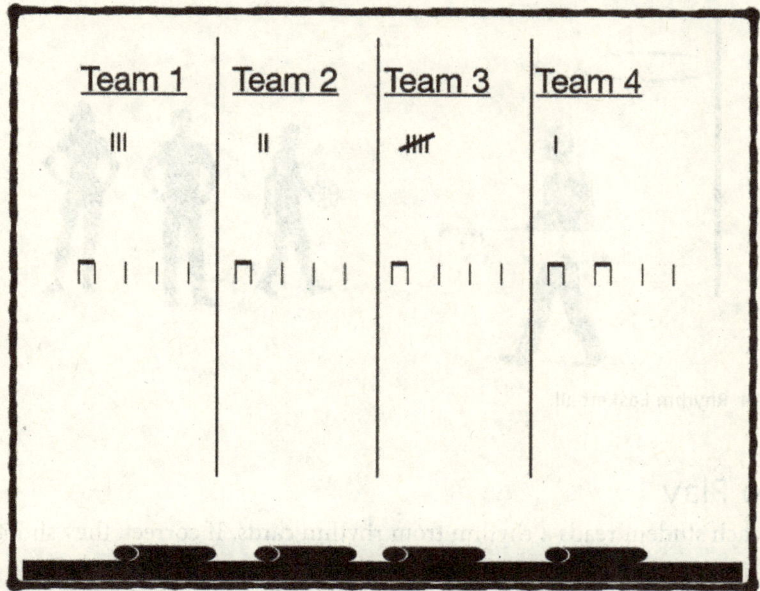

FIGURE 13.3 Chalkboard setup for Rhythm Race.

Rhythm Basketball

This game gives students a chance to show their rhythm reading skills independently. Older students will ask for this game again and again as they become more confident and competitive.

Objectives

- Review known rhythms.
- Nonmusical: Build class identity.
- Nonmusical: Build excitement and expend some energy.

Materials

- Appropriate rhythm cards with rhythms students have learned in class.
- A small toy basketball hoop (a clean bucket or garbage can works, too).
- A small bean bag or small plush toy (crumpled up paper can be substituted).

Setup

- Group size: 6–30 students (best with about 12–16).
- Two lines of students facing the basketball hoop.
- Teacher stands near hoop facing students and holds several rhythm cards.

FIGURE 13.4 Rhythm Basketball.

How to Play

In short, each student reads a rhythm from rhythm cards. If correct, they shoot a basket to earn points for their team.

1. Show a rhythm card to the first person in line. That student reads it while keeping the beat.
2. If correct, they get to shoot a basket. If they make the basket, the team gets two points.
3. If they miss the basket, they get no points.
4. If they don't get the rhythm correct, they do not get to shoot a basket.
5. Play continues to the first person in the other line and alternates between the teams.

Variation

Put tape or other markers on the floor at varying distances to the basket. Students get a choice of how far from the basket they want to shoot: close, medium, and far. If they choose the "far" tape mark, they read only one card. If they choose the "close," they read eight cards. Again, all rhythms must be perfectly executed without hesitating, keeping a steady beat. This variation allows students who are better at shooting baskets to opt to do fewer rhythms and those who are worse at shooting baskets to opt to do more rhythms to make an easier shot!

14

Games to Practice Musical Elements

Introduction

These rhythm and melody games are for after the first 3 weeks. They build on previous games and add new challenges. They also require more knowledge from the students and the foundation the teachers set in the first few weeks.

More Fun with Flash cards

Objectives

- Review rhythmic and melodic reading.
- Increase the tempo of a lesson.

Materials

- Pitch flashcards or rhythm flashcards.
- A music stand (optional).

Setup

- Group size: 3–50 students.
- Lecture setup, teacher with flashcards in the front with students facing the cards.
- Flashcards in the teacher's hands or on a music stand.

How to Play

In short, the teacher shows flash cards and the students read them.

Your First Year as an Elementary Music Teacher. Andrew S. Paney, Oxford University Press. © Oxford University Press 2025.
DOI: 10.1093/oso/9780197631430.003.0014

1. Choose cards that include only elements that the students have already learned. This is a *practicing* activity, not a learning activity. You want them to build familiarity and speed with reading.
2. Show the first card and count it in: "one, two, three, read." You may need to point to each beat the first few times you read cards with your students, but after that, they should read it without your help.
3. As soon as they finish one card, flip it over and reveal the next card, immediately counting it in so there is no gap between the cards.
4. Continue until you have reached the end of the selected cards or until you or the students are ready to move on.

Variation: Around the World

1. Hold 20 or more cards in your hands (again, all cards that include only rhythms your students know).
2. Go to one student and ask them to read the card while keeping the beat. Tell them that they can go as fast or slow as they'd like, but the beat needs to be consistent.
3. If they get it correct, don't say anything, just hand them the card.
4. If they don't get it correct, have the next student read it. Continue until somebody reads it correctly and give the card to that person.
5. Move to the next card and continue until you run out of cards.
6. Ask, "Raise your hand if you have one or more cards. Raise your hand if you have two or more cards." Etc. Just a small acknowledgment of people is enough, there doesn't need to be a winner.

Rhythm Down the Lane

This quiet game is a favorite of students and is similar to the Telephone game. This game is a great way to fill some time when a lesson runs short! The set up and materials are exactly the same as Rhythm Race.

Objectives

- Review known rhythms.
- Build musical memory.
- Nonmusical: Build class identity.

Materials

- Marker board or chalkboard.
- 2–5 dry erase markers or chalk pieces, one for each team.
- Optional: Appropriate rhythm cards (ones that include only rhythms students have learned).

Setup

- Group size: 6–30 students (ages 9 and up).
- 2–5 lines of students facing the board, 3-6 students in each line.
- Classroom and board setup are the same as Rhythm Race (see Figures 13.1 and 13.2).

How to Play

In short, students pass a rhythm down a line by tapping it on the shoulder of the person in front of them. The last person writes the rhythm on the board.

1. Show a 4-beat rhythm card only to the student at the back of each line. Each student memorizes the rhythm card and waits.
2. Say, "Begin!" Each student pats the rhythm on the shoulder of the person in front of him. That student then pats the rhythm on the shoulder of the person in front of her, until the rhythm gets to the front of the line. The rhythm passes with pats only and with no verbal explanations or utterances.
3. The person in the front of the line, the last to receive the rhythm, writes the rhythm on the board using traditional or stick notation (See "Rhythm Race" step 2 in Chapter 13 to compare traditional and stick notation).
4. Ask each group to clap what their group wrote on the board.
5. Show the group the card that represents the correct rhythm and ask, "Does your answer match?"
6. Award points for each correct answer.
7. The student who wrote on the board goes to the end of her line and play begins again.

Rhythm Baseball

This is a more involved game and takes a little more time. I like to use it as a reward at the end of class when appropriate. Like Rhythm Basketball, each student gets to perform rhythms on their own.

Objectives

- Review known rhythms.
- Nonmusical: Build class identity.
- Nonmusical: Build excitement and expend some energy.

Materials

- Appropriate rhythm cards, cards that include only rhythms students have learned in class.
- Chairs or other items that can serve as bases.

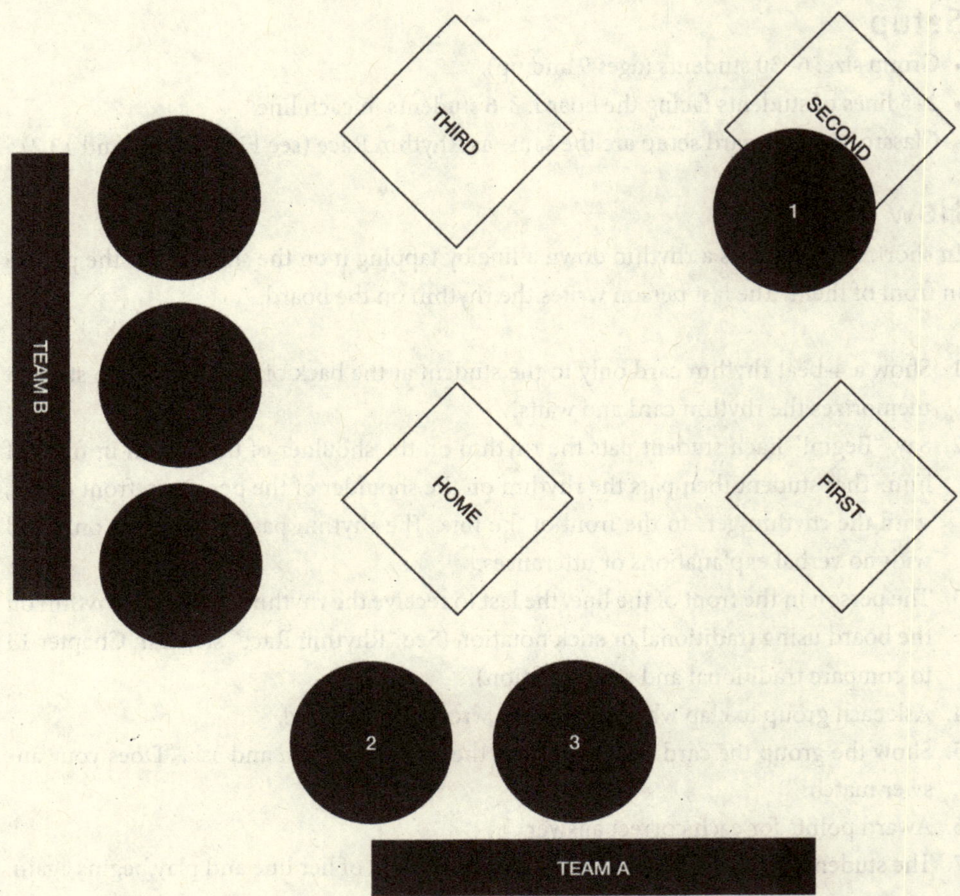

FIGURE 14.1 Set up for Rhythm Baseball. The numbered players are "at bat." Player 1 is on second base and player 2 is about to take their turn.

Setup

- Group size: 6–30 students.
- Four chairs set up in a square, marking first base, second base, third base, and home plate (see Figure 14.1).
- Two teams, each in a line along the side lines (one stretching from home plate toward first base and the other from home plate to third base).

How to Play

In short, each student chooses how much they want to read, attempts it, and takes bases if correct.

1. The first team "at bat" sends their first batter to home plate.
2. Ask the batter: "Do you want to go for a single, double, triple, or home run?" The student chooses.

3. Choosing a single means they will read just *one* rhythm card and advance to first base (if performed perfectly).
4. Double means *two* rhythm cards and advancing to second base.
5. Triple means *four* rhythm cards and advancing to third base.
6. Home run means *eight* rhythm cards and advancing to home plate, by rounding all the bases.
7. The student performs the rhythm.
8. The person at bat should keep the beat audibly, by clapping or patting.
9. The rhythm should be performed orally on rhythm syllables (e.g., "*ta tadi ta ta*").
10. Judge the student's reading very strictly! Do not allow hesitating on a rhythm or cutting a rest short. This will increase the excitement of the game and make it consistent across players.
11. If a student's performance is perfect, the student "runs the bases" by walking and touching each base and staying on the base he chose (e.g., if he chose a single, he stays on first base).
12. If a student's performance has even a small error, tell them where it is and the team get "an out."
13. Repeat with the next batter up.

Some Notes

- Teams only gain points for players who make it to home base (who "make a run").
- As in real baseball, if you have a runner on third and the batter hits a triple, the runner will be forced home.
- There is no stealing bases or advancing in bases without being forced to the next one by another runner.
- Teams get an "out" only for mistakes in reading. I don't use "strikes" when I play the game.
- Make clear what the point limit is for each inning. I usually limit teams to three runs or two outs before the other team is at bat.
- Strategy: If a team has two points and the limit is three points per inning, they may want to stack the bases and then go for a grand slam to earn some bonus points. Then, instead of getting three points, they could earn 6 points (four runners in on the grand slam).

Music Memory Match

Objectives

- Practice reading melodic elements.
- Build excitement and enjoyment of music class.

Materials

- Eight pairs of melodic flashcards. Make your own or use ▶ Visual 16.5 in Appendix A.
- Pitch instrument (piano, tuning fork, guitar, phone, etc.)

Setup

- Group size: 2–25 students.
- Open floor space of about 4 feet by 4 feet.

How to Play

In short, students choose and perform two flashcards and keep them if they match.

1. Have students read all sixteen rhythm flashcards together. As they read each one, place it upside down on the floor in a four-by-four grid.
2. Divide the class into two teams and have them make two lines where they can each see the playing space.
3. Choose the first person in one of the lines to be first. That person will choose one card from the playing board and read it aloud while keeping a beat. If they read it correctly, they get to choose a second card and read that card the same way. If both cards match, the student takes the cards for their team and immediately takes another turn. If they do not match, they turn the cards back over and the other team takes a turn.
4. Alternate teams until all cards are claimed.

Some Notes

- It helps to have all students on one side of the playing space, so everyone can read the rhythm with the right side up.
- Ask students to turn the card over while keeping it on the floor in the exact same spot in the grid. This will help others to be able to read it, too, and to know where it is when it is their turn.

Melodic Variation

You can do this game with melodic flashcards, too. Just be sure to give the key or starting pitch to keep everyone singing in the same key for the game. You may need to repeat the pitch several times throughout the game. You can use melodic flash cards for "More Fun with Flash Cards," "Rhythm Down the Lane," and "Rhythm Baseball," too.

Poison (Melody)

This is an easy game that requires very few, if any, materials. I like to use it regularly as a fun break for my students.

Objectives

- Review known solfège syllables and pitches.
- Practice pitches.
- Practice pitches in newer contexts.

Materials

- Pitch instrument.
- Marker board (optional).

Setup

- Group size: 6–80 students.

How to Play

In short, you sing short melodic patterns and students sing them back. They listen for a particular pattern that they aren't allowed to sing. They get a point if they avoid saying the "poison" pattern and you get a point if they don't.

1. The first time you play it say, "Echo me," and sing a short, 4-beat melodic pattern in solfège. For example, you might sing "*so mi re do*" on quarter notes. Your students immediately echo you.
2. Do the same with three or four more patterns, ending with the poison pattern twice.
3. Say, "Sing that pattern again." They sing it. "Let's make that our poison pattern. You sing back everything I sing *except* that particular pattern. Let's do an example."
4. Do several patterns and then do the poison motive. If the room is completely quiet, give the students a point. If there is any sound at all, even just the start of a word, you take the point.
5. I usually play to three points and start another game if there is time and students are still enjoying it.

Some Notes

- I love this game for practicing melodic patterns. For instance, if a song has a *so-re-mi* that students consistently sing incorrectly. I will make sure they sing *so-re-mi* during this game over and over again. The students think that I'm trying to trick them to get a point, but really I'm using the game to give them lots of musical practice.
- You can make many variations of this game. Some that I like to make it a little harder are, in order of difficulty:
  - Sing in solfège with hand signs.
  - Sing in solfège with hand signs while keeping a beat with the other hand.
  - Increase the tempo.
  - Increase the length of the pattern from 4 beats to 8.
  - Change the meter to 6:8.
  - Hum and show hand signs while students respond with hand signs and singing the solfège.
  - Hum and *don't* show hand signs while students respond with hand signs and singing the solfège.

- Show only hand signs and don't sing while students respond with hand signs and singing.
- Show a printed 4-beat pattern that students read for 4 beats then immediately sing with hand signs and solfège (can be staff notation or stick notation).

Staff Jumping (Melody)

Objectives

- Review staff rules.
- Review notes on the staff.

Materials

- A large staff on the floor. Make one with painter's tape or use a music rug.

Setup

- Group size: 3 to 5, with as many additional students as active observers.

How to Play

In short, students respond to actions called by the teacher by moving to the appropriate line or space on the floor staff.

1. Stand on the staff yourself with students standing around the staff, preferably all on the "bottom" of the staff, so nobody is reading it upside down.
2. Ask, "am I standing on a line or in a space?" After students respond, ask, "How about now?" Repeat this process two or three times as students yell out their answers (no hand-raising).
3. "I'd like two of you to try showing lines or spaces." Get two volunteers and have them stand on the staff.
4. Call out "line" or "space" and students jump to that space.

Some Notes

- You can use this same game to give students practice in:
  - Naming notes on the treble clef (or bass or any other clef).
  - Showing intervals ("show me a third starting on D").
  - Practicing solfège/scale degrees. Put a marker for *do* on the staff and ask them to jump to *re*, *so*, *ti*, etc.
- Add some interest by adding a competition element to it. Here are some options:
  - Have two people race to get three points by getting to the line or the space before the other person.
  - Divide the class into two teams and play teams, rotating who is playing for each team.
  - If you don't want to use teams, the first person to answer correctly (get to the correct spot on the staff) gets to stay on the staff, and the other person (or persons) rotate off the staff while new people come in.

PART IV

Complete Lessons for Weeks 1–3

15

Early Elementary Lessons (Grades Pre-K, Kindergarten, and 1)

Introduction

Young children in grades Pre-K, kindergarten, and 1 are going to enter your room with excitement and joy. These lessons are designed to channel that glee into positive, collaborative music making.

How to Teach These Lessons Well

In the first three music days (which may occur over three weeks or in any other combination) you want to establish the routines for your classroom. The most important goals for these lessons are:

- Class will begin in an orderly way; each person will go immediately to his or her assigned seat.
- Everyone will contribute to the class in a productive, respectful way.
- Joyful music making will happen every class period.
- Singing will happen every time.
- Class will end in an orderly way, with the same "goodbye" song and a quiet room.
- If any problems arise, you will deal with them in a respectful and predetermined way.

As mentioned in Chapter 5 (see Appendix B), each lesson for early childhood children is arranged in Three Acts. This allows you to keep things moving quickly to avoid students' minds wandering or for them to start chatting with their neighbors. Each Act

Your First Year as an Elementary Music Teacher. Andrew S. Paney, Oxford University Press. © Oxford University Press 2025.
DOI: 10.1093/oso/9780197631430.003.0015

FIGURE 15.1 The suggested range for songs sung at the beginning of the year for students in pre-K, kindergarten, and grade 1.

has a focus and a particular objective. Act I starts with the children seated, Act II includes standing activities and songs, and Act III concludes with seated songs and activities.

Remember to minimize transition time! Aim for less than one second from the moment you finish one song or activity until you start the next one. This will keep your students engaged, ensuring they stay with *your* fun, instead of creating their own.

All of these lessons have been designed to be successful in any classroom, with or without technology or other resources. If you have resources, though, feel free to use them!

Each lesson ends with Extensions. These are easy ways to add to the lesson, if you complete the lesson before the class period ends.

Always sing songs in pitch ranges that *students* can sing. Neither you nor I enjoy singing outside of our range. To make sure your students don't have to experience that discomfort, choose appropriate keys for each song. Use a pitch device (piano, guitar, recorder, tuning fork, or even your phone) every time!

Lesson 1: Setting the Tone

The first day is important and gives you the chance to set the tone for a joyful, orderly, musical experience each time you see your students. Put time into practicing your lesson for the first day. Know it so well that you can improvise when things don't go as expected.

Objectives (What you want to accomplish today) Students will:

- Demonstrate classroom procedures (rules, seating charts).
- Experience a joyful, music-filled lesson.
- Sing new and known songs.
- Respond to music by moving in appropriate ways.

Materials (Don't forget to bring):

- Your filled-in seating chart. (See Chapter 3 for information on how to create one.)
- For Pre-K and kindergarten: A poster with an ear and a singing mouth ("Listen and Sing"). See ▶Visual 15.1 in Appendix A.

- For Grade 1: A poster with your class expectations. Mine says, "Show Respect; Follow Directions; Do Your Best." (See Chapter 4 for more about expectations.) See Visual 15.2 in Appendix A.
- A pitch instrument (piano, tuning fork, or an app on your phone)
- Cow puppet or small stuffed plush. You can also use a printed picture of a cow. See Visual 15.3 in Appendix A.
- Canvas bag. This will be where you keep and hide your materials (like the cow puppet).

Songs and Other Music (Review these before the lesson, See Appendix B)

- "Fishy, Fishy in the Brook" rhyme (see Appendix B) (all songs and rhymes are printed in Appendix B).
- "Peas Porridge Hot" rhyme (see Appendix B).
- "Teddy Bear, Teddy Bear" song; Starting pitch A (Key of D, see Appendix B).
- "Bingo" song; Starting pitch D (Key of G, see Appendix B).
- "Bow Wow Wow" song; Starting pitch D (Key of D, see Appendix B).
- "Ring Around the Rosie" song; Starting pitch A (Key of D, see Appendix B).
- "Johnny Works with One Hammer" song; Starting pitch D (Key of D, see Appendix B).
- "A E I O U La Vaca eres tú" rhyme (see Appendix B).
- "Firefly" song; Starting pitch A (Key of D, see Appendix B).

National Standards

- MU:Cr1.1.PK.a—With substantial guidance, explore and experience a variety of music.
- MU:Cr1.1.K.a—With guidance, explore and experience music concepts (such as beat and melodic contour).
- MU:Cr1.1.1.a—With limited guidance, create musical ideas (such as answering a musical question) for a specific purpose.

Procedures

Act I: Seated Music and Getting Settled

1. Introduction and assign seats.
    a. Say, "Thank you for entering quietly and sitting on the rug." As students enter, instruct them where to go before you assign their seats.
    b. Assign seats. Say, "Listen as I call your name and sit where I ask." Call each child's name, using your premade seating chart, as you stand by the chair where they will sit. Remind students to remain sitting quietly as you complete this task, "Thanks for sitting quietly as we find everyone's seat."
2. Activity: "Do What I Do."
    a. As soon as all seats are assigned, Say, "Do what I do," and immediately begin patting both your shoulders. Switch the motion every few seconds by patting a different part of your body, keeping a beat, without talking. This is a time of doing something together without making a sound (or making a very quiet sound).

b. Vary your movements. Here are some ideas: Pat your head, ears, chin, shoulders, elbows, chest, hips, knees, etc.; touch two finger tips together; slide your hands back and forth on each other to make a soft swish sound; point to your smile; point to your frown; point in the air.

3. Rules and Expectations
   a. For kindergarten and younger students: Teach rules and expectations for class. Say, "In music we listen and sing." Show the motions for each and ask students to say it alone. "When I am talking, you . . ." gesture to show listening. "When I am singing, you . . ." gesture to show listening. Plan to use the hand motions *every* time you talk about the expectations for these students. This will help you to give nonverbal reminders in future class meetings. If you choose to, you can print Visual 15.1 in Appendix A as a visual aid for this part of the lesson.
   b. For Grade 1 students: Teach rules and expectations for class. I use: Show Respect, Follow Directions, and Do Your Best (see Chapter 4). Say, "In music class we will follow some simple rules." Spend some time on each and give examples of appropriate and inappropriate behavior: "In music class, we . . ." and "In music class we don't . . ." This should take no more than 2 minutes. Because first graders are growing in their reading skills, I recommend posting the text of your expectations as a visual aid in your classroom, see Visual 15.3 in Appendix A.
4. Rhyme: "Fishy, Fishy in the Brook."
   a. Say, "Show me how you can make a fish with your two hands" (mime a swimming fish by putting your palms together and wiggling it back and forth and forward and back). Say, "Listen" and say the rhyme while doing the four motions.
   b. Repeat it. Say, "Listen again and do the motions with me." Say the rhyme a second time by yourself (it's OK if some students join you—they probably will!).
   c. Review the words. Say, "What am I pretending to be when I move my hands like this?" Students: "You're pretending to be a swimming fish." Say, "What about when I do this?" Ask for each motion and help them if they don't know.
   d. Say the rhyme together. Say, "Say the rhyme with me again" and say the rhyme and do the motions together and then go immediately into the next activity.
5. Rhyme: "Peas Porridge Hot."
   a. Say, "Listen" and say the whole rhyme for them while keeping a beat with both hands on your lap.
   b. Review the words. Ask, "How can we show that something is 'hot' with our hands? Show me with your hands." Choose somebody's motion. Ask. "How can we show that something is 'cold' with our hands? Show me with your hands." Choose somebody's motion. Ask "What about 'nine days old?' "
   c. Review the motions. Model the motions for your students and say, "You do the motions while I say the rhyme again." Say the rhyme while you and the students do the motions.
   d. Say the rhyme together. Say, "Say it with me this time." Repeat the rhyme and motions with the students.

Act II: Standing Music

1. Sing "Teddy Bear."
   a. Say, "Do what I do"; sing and do all the motions for "Teddy Bear." Say, "Sing it with me this time." Sing the song and do the motions while the students join you.
   b. Students sing. Say, "Now you sing it by yourselves." Do the motions, but don't sing. It's ok if they can't make it through on their own—don't rescue them! Just say, "Let's try it again together!"
2. Sing "Bingo."
   a. Say, "listen to this song and clap when I say a letter." Sing "Bingo" and model clapping on the "B I N G O" part.
   b. Sing together. Say, "Sing with me this time" and sing it again with them, still clapping on the letters.
   c. Put the letters in your head. Say, "This time let's sing the B just in our heads, not out loud." Repeat putting one more letter "in your head" each time until all letters are gone.
3. Sing "Bow Wow Wow."
   a. Say, "Do what I do; listen, but don't sing." Sing "Bow Wow Wow" and do motions: On the first phrase, step in place three times; on the second phrase, bend over and shake your finger as if scolding a small dog; on the third phrase, turn around in place slowly; on the final phrase, step in place three times.
   b. Sing it together. Say, "Sing it with me this time" and sing it again with the students while doing the motions.
   c. Say, "Let's do that again and see if I do anything different at the end of the song." Sing it again with students and do all motions, but add a clap after the last word (on the final beat of rest).
4. Sing "Ring around the Rosie."
   a. Say, "Stand up and move your feet like this." Model stepping in place. Say, "Listen to this song—it's a little different from the one you know!" Get your starting pitch and sing the song for them as you step the beat. Since many students know this song, give a big ritardando at the end as you sing "all fall UP!" and stand on your tiptoes.
   b. Sing it together. Repeat and invite students to sing with you as you end the song with: "All fall UP," "All fall halfway down," "All fall to the side" (lean slightly to one side), and the last time, "All sit down."

Act III: Seated Music

1. Sing "Johnny Works with One Hammer."
   a. Say, "Everyone take out your imaginary hammer" (mime taking a hammer out of your pocket and start hammering on the beat). Say, "Listen," and sing the song as you all keep the beat with your imaginary hammers.
   b. Add verse two. After the last line, ask, "How can we show two hammers?" Sing the second verse, with everyone keeping the beat with two hammers. Repeat the same process for each new verse.

2. Say "A E I O U La Vaca eres tú."
   a. Ask students to put both hands on one knee. Have them pat the beat with both hands on the same knee, alternating knees. Say the rhyme twice while you and the students pat both hands on alternating knees.
   b. Check understanding. Ask, "Does anyone know what a 'vaca' is?" Allow students to respond and tell them that it means "cow" if they don't tell you. Bring a small stuffed cow out of your bag and put it on one knee. Say the rhyme again, moving the cow from knee to knee in the same way you patted each knee previously.
   c. Guessing game. Ask, "Which knee do you think the cow will land on this time?" Students choose one. Do the rhyme again and ask them if they guessed correctly. Repeat once or twice.
3. Briefly review expectations.
   a. Remind students of your expectations for the next class period: Enter the room quietly, sit in your assigned seat, and follow class rules.
   b. Say, "I'm looking for someone who can tell me our classroom rules. Raise your hand if you can." Call on one child who is modeling correct behavior (sitting quietly and raising a hand).
   c. Review the purpose of expectations. Say, "It's important to me that we each treat each other and the instruments and other items in this room well. This will help each of you to have a wonderful music class every time I see you!"
4. Sing, "Firefly." Say, "Listen," and sing the "Firefly" song (or your chosen closing song). Say, "Listen again and this time whisper 'Good night, firefly,' with me at the end." Sing the song and invite students to whisper with you.

Extensions

1. Echo body percussion.
2. Play "Do What I do."
3. Whisper rhymes from earlier in the lesson ("Peas Porridge Hot," "Fishy Fishy," "Teddy Bear").

Lesson 2: Building Excitement

The hardest part, the first lesson, is out of the way. Now you want to build on your foundation and reinforce your routines and build students' excitement about coming to music class. Familiarity is important to young students and for this reason, you will do many of the same songs and activities you did in Lesson 1. I aim to have 20%–40% new material in each lesson. We will slightly modify how we do songs, games, and activities that they learned last class.

Objectives (What you want to accomplish today):

- Reinforce classroom procedures (rules, seating charts).
- Students will sing new and known songs and rhymes.
- Students will make higher sounds with their voices.

Materials (Don't forget to bring):

- Your filled-in seating chart.
- A pitch instrument (piano, tuning fork, or an app on your phone).
- Visual aids for "Who's That Knocking at My Window," papers with two animals on each (Cow and Frog, Toucan and Penguin, Horse and Llama, etc.). See Visual 15.4.
- Cow puppet or small stuffed plush. You can also use a printed picture of a cow. See Visual 15.3.
- Owl puppet or small stuffed plush. You can also use a printed picture of an owl. See Visual 15.5.
- Canvas bag to hide puppets or stuffed animals.

Songs and Other Music

- "Fishy, Fishy in the Brook" rhyme (all songs and rhymes are printed in Appendix B).
- "Johnny Works with One Hammer" song; Starting pitch D (Key of D).
- New: "Who's That Knocking?" song; Starting pitch D (Key of D).[1]
- "Teddy Bear, Teddy Bear" song; Starting pitch A (Key of D).
- New: "Bluebells, Cockle Shells" song; Starting pitch A (Key of D).[2]
- New: "Ickle Ockle Blue Bottle" song; Starting pitch A (Key of D).[3]
- "A E I O U La Vaca eres tú" rhyme.
- New: "Starlight, Star Bright" song: Starting pitch A (Key of D).[4]
- "Firefly" song; Starting pitch A (Key of D).

National Standards

- MU:Cr2.1.PK.a—With substantial guidance, explore favorite musical ideas (such as movements, vocalizations, or instrumental accompaniments).
- MU:Cr2.1.K.a—With guidance, demonstrate and choose favorite musical ideas.
- MU:Cr2.1.1.a—With limited guidance, demonstrate and discuss personal reasons for selecting musical ideas that represent expressive intent.

Procedures

Act I: Seated Music

1. Lead "Do What I Do." Say, "Do what I do" and immediately begin patting both your shoulders. Continue to switch the motion regularly. Look at each child and mentally assess how they are responding: Are they interested? Happy? Bored? Adjust your motions based on visual feedback.

2. Say "Fishy Fishy in the Brook." Say, "Put your hands together" and mime a swimming fish. Take a breath or give a gesture that you're starting and say the rhyme together. Repeat the rhyme in a different voice (mama, daddy, baby, whisper voice, etc.).
3. Review Expectations. Say, "In music we listen and sing." Show the motions for each and ask students to say it alone. "When I am talking, you . . ." gesture to show listening. "When I am singing, you . . ." gesture to show listening. "When we sing together, you . . ." gesture to show singing.
4. Sing "Johnny Works with One Hammer." Say, "Let me see your hammers" (mime taking a hammer out of your pocket and start hammering on the beat). Say, "Sing with me" and sing the full song as you all keep the beat with your imaginary hammers. If your students are engaged, try letting them fill in the last word ("Then he works with ___") without you.
5. Sing "Who's That Knocking at My Window?" Say, "Listen," and sing the first part of the song for them: "Who's that knocking at my window? Who's that knocking at my door?" Near the end of the first part, pull out Visual 15.4. Sing the second part naming the two animals: "Roosters knocking at my window; Penguins knocking at my door." Repeat with as many sheets you've created. I recommend at least three and not more than six.

Act II: Standing Music

1. Sing "Teddy Bear." Say, "Sing with me," and sing the song while doing all the motions. Repeat only if students seem interested. If you repeat, say, "I want to hear if you can sing the whole song without me." Let them sing the whole song while you do the motions with them (but don't sing). Don't rescue them, just keep doing the motions and help them get back on track!
2. Sing "Bluebells, Cockle Shells."
   a. Say, "Listen," and sing the song, including chanting the names of the months at the end. Say, "Listen again and say the months of the year with me." Sing the song by yourself and gesture for students to say the months with you (you may need to say them somewhat slowly).
   b. Add motions to "Bluebells, Cockle Shells." Say, "Sing the song with me this time and bend your knees when we say your birthday month. My birthday is in <April>, so I will say, 'January, February, March, April, May . . .' and crouch down on 'April.' Let's try it together!" Do the song and chant the months together. No need to repeat it again in this lesson.
3. Sing "Ickle Ockle Blue Bottle." Say, "Do what I do and listen." Sing the song while stepping in place. On the last word, stop stepping and put out your two hands with palms up (as if carrying a large tray in front of yourself). Ask, "On what word did I freeze?" If they can't answer, repeat the first step. If they answer correctly, invite them to sing the song with you while following your motions (stepping in place and freezing while putting out your two hands on the last word). Say, "There's an animal in this song. What is it? Let's show a fish with our hands in the first part of the song." Sing the song while

stepping in place and moving your hands like a fish. Still freeze on the last word with your hands extended.

Act III: Seated Music

1. Say "A E I O U La Vaca Eres Tu."
   a. Say the rhyme twice. Then say, "A E I O U," and pause to see if they finish it. If not, say the rest of the rhyme for them.
   b. Add movement to "A E I O U." Pat your right knee with both hands, then your left knee, alternating on each beat. Invite students to say it with you.
   c. Ask, "What is a 'vaca'?" Students answer "a cow." "Yes, 'vaca' is Spanish for cow. I brought my cow again today." Take out the cow and ask, "What does A E I O U mean?" students answer or help them understand vowels in Spanish. Say, "This rhyme is in Spanish and the words mean 'A E I O U the cow is you!"
   d. Play the game again, inviting students to guess on which knee the cow will end the rhyme (you can control where the cow will land because he will always end on the same side on which he started). Play the game 2–3 times.
2. Vocal Exploration with Mr. Owl.
   a. Say hello to Mr. Owl. Say, "I brought a little friend with me today, but he's probably sleeping." Reach into your bag to pull out a small owl puppet. Say, "Oh, he's awake! This is Mr. Owl. Can you say hello to him, please?" Students say hello. Say, "I'm so sorry! I forgot to tell you that he only speaks owl. Does anyone know how to say hello in owl?" A child offers a hooting sound. "Yes! How did you know? Let's all try to say hello like that." Everyone hoots like the child did.
   b. Say goodbye to Mr. Owl. Say, "Let's learn another phrase in Owl. I'm going to teach you how to say Goodbye. You say goodbye like this," give a different hoot pattern that you think you can remember. Be sure to use a sound that is high enough to be in the students' head voice, higher than C5 on the piano. Say, "Mr. Owl is looking very sleepy, let's say goodbye to him and let him go back to sleep." Students hoot their new goodbye pattern and you put Mr. Owl away in your bag.
3. Sing "Starlight Star Bright." Say, "Listen," and sing "Starlight Star Bright." Choose some simple hand motions that you can use each time. Say, "Sing with me this time," and sing the song again.
4. Sing "Firefly." Say, "Sing with me," and sing the "Firefly" song, whispering "Goodnight firefly" at the end. If it feels appropriate, do the song one more time before ending the lesson.

Extensions

1. Echo body percussion.
2. Review the activities you did today, "The first thing we did in music today was ______. Raise your hand if you can tell me what we did next."
3. Sing a song for them, one you know well and like.

Lesson 3: Giving Ownership

Your students are starting to understand what music class with you will be like. Keep building on the patterns and routines you've established and continue to give ownership to your students. In this lesson, you'll allow them to make more decisions and to establish their class identity. Laughing together is a great way to build a safe and collaborative environment!

Objectives (What you want to accomplish today):

- Students will sing new and known songs and rhymes.
- Students will suggest appropriate movements to fit with music.
- Students will move their voices higher and lower.
- Students will move their bodies to music.

Materials (Don't forget to bring):

- Your filled-in seating chart.
- A pitch instrument (piano, tuning fork, or an app on your phone).
- Visual aid for "One Two Three Four, Mary at the Kitchen Door," one sheet of paper with a door on one side and a gate on the other side.
- Visual aids for "Who's That Knocking at My Window," papers with two animals on each (Cow and Frog, Toucan and Penguin, Horse and Llama, etc.). See Visual 15.4.
- Owl puppet or small stuffed plush. You can also use a printed picture of an owl. See Visual 15.5.
- Crocodile and Dog puppets or small stuffed animals. These can be any two contrasting animals. If you don't have any stuffed animals/plushes, buy a couple that are between four and six inches tall.
- Canvas bag to hide puppets or stuffed animals.

Songs and Other Music

- New: "One Two Three Four, Mary at the Kitchen Door" rhyme[5] (all songs and rhymes are printed in Appendix B).
- "Starlight, Star Bright" song: Starting pitch A (Key of D).
- "Bluebell, Cockle Shells" song; Starting pitch A (Key of D).
- "Ickle Ockle Blue Bottle" song; Starting pitch A (Key of D).
- "Bow Wow Wow" song; Starting pitch D (Key of D).
- New: "Frosty Weather" song; Starting pitch A (Key of D).[6]
- "Peas Porridge Hot" rhyme.
- "Who's That Knocking?" song; Starting pitch D (Key of D).
- New: "Rain, Rain, Go Away" song; Starting pitch A (Key of D).[7]
- "Firefly" song; Starting pitch A (Key of D).

National Standards

- MU:Cr2.1.PK.a—With substantial guidance, explore favorite musical ideas (such as movements, vocalizations, or instrumental accompaniments).
- MU:Cr2.1.K.a—With guidance, demonstrate and choose favorite musical ideas.
- MU:Cr2.1.1.a—With limited guidance, demonstrate and discuss personal reasons for selecting musical ideas that represent expressive intent.

Procedures

Act I: Seated Music

1. Lead "Do What I Do."
   a. Say, "Do what I do," and immediately begin patting both your shoulders. Continue to switch the motion regularly.
   b. Add children's leading. Look at children and choose something they are doing and imitate it: "I see that Maria is patting her head with just one hand. Let's all try that!" Invite Maria to lead the class in moving in other ways. You may need to remind the children of the kinds of things you led: "Remember that we patted our heads, rubbed our hands together, smiled, and pointed up and down. Watch Maria to see what she chooses to do next."
2. Rules and Expectations. Say, "Last time you did a great job following our class rules. You listened and sang. Can you show me how you listen and sing?" Show hand motions for each. Briefly review how to implement the rules in class, "If I'm talking, you should be . . ." Student respond that they should be listening. "If I'm singing, you should be . . . ." "If we're all singing, you should be . . . ."
3. Say, "One Two Three Four Mary at the Kitchen Door."
   a. Ask, "where is Mary first?" "Where is she after that?" "Say the rhyme with me this time." Say the rhyme with students.
   b. Repeat "One Two Three Four Mary at the Kitchen Door" with variation. Try different tempos, giving a story for each. For instance, "Mary is very tired and it is taking her a long time to get to the door. How would she say the rhyme?" Or "Mary just drank her coffee and is zipping around. How would she say the rhyme?" Ask, "I want to know if you can say that rhyme by yourselves." They say the rhyme while looking at your pictures.
4. Vocal Exploration with Mr. Owl. Say, "Mr. Owl is waking up a little and wants to hear if you remember your two phrases in Owl." Bring out the owl puppet and invite students to say "hello" and "goodbye" in Owl. Say, "Today we're going to learn how to say, 'I love to sing.' This is a longer one! I hope we can do it!" Give a slightly longer hoot pattern with slides and that helps them use their head voices. Be sure to choose a pattern you can remember! After students practice it a couple times, have them say goodbye to Mr. Owl "in Owl" and put him back in the bag to sleep.

5. Sing "Starlight Star Bright."
   a. Say, "Sing with me," and sing the song while doing hand motions. Be sure to start it in an appropriate key for students to use their singing voices (above A4).
   b. Say, "Let's sing the song quietly again to make sure Mr. Owl has fallen completely asleep, wherever he is."

Act II: Standing Music

1. Sing "Bluebells, Cockle Shells." Say, "Sing with me!" and start the song. Go directly into chanting the months and crouch down on your own birth month. If necessary, clarify how the crouching works: "When we say your birthday month, bend your knees" and do it once more together. Unless your students are really into this one, move on in the lesson plan. If you think they'd like to do it again, give them one change in how you do it. For instance, have them go on their tiptoes when their month is said.
2. Sing "Ickle Ockle Blue Bottle."
   a. Say, "Sing with me," and sing the song while doing the motions (walking in place, fish movement with hands, and freezing on the last word with your palms extended).
   b. Add "Ickle Ockle Blue Bottle" movement. Say, "This is our fishbowl," and point to the boundaries where you want students to stay (they can be quite small). "While I sing the song, I will swim around the fishbowl like this." Sing with the same motions, but moving your feet around the "fishbowl."
   c. Transition out of "Ickle Ockle Blue Bottle." Say, "This last time, let's swim until all our feet are on the outside of the rug." Help students move to a standing circle.
3. Sing "Bow Wow Wow."
   a. Say, "Do what I do and sing with me." Sing and do the motions to the song while students join you. Say, "Last time I did something different at the very end of the song. What was it?" Students tell you that you clapped at the end.
   b. Add more motions to "Bow Wow Wow." Say, "Let's all clap after the last Bow Wow Wow part." Sing the song with motions and on the last beat, on the final rest, clap and jump turn 180 degrees so you're facing the opposite direction. Say, "What did I do differently that time?" Students explain that you turned around. Ask, "When did I turn around?" Students respond that you turned on the clap. Say, "Lets sing that again and jump on the clap at the end." Sing the song together again, repeating it immediately so that you sing it facing out of the circle, then immediately jump to face the inside again.
4. Sing "Frosty Weather." With everyone standing in a circle, say, "Listen and do what I do." Sing the song and do the actions (walk in place until the word "when," freeze on that word, take small steps toward the center of the circle on the last line, "we all go together"). Say, "This time, instead of 'we all go together,' let's sing 'those wearing blue go together.'" Sing the song and only those wearing blue take small steps in on the last phrase. Repeat with different colors.

Act III: Seated Music

1. Say "Peas porridge hot." Say, "Say this rhyme with me," and say the rhyme while showing the motions students chose. Say it just one more time, but gesture for them to complete each line without you saying it: "Peas porridge _____; Peas porridge ______; Peas porridge in a ___________; Some like it _____; some like it ______; some like it in a ____________" (note that you may need to wait a few seconds for students to fill in the word or to understand what you're doing; they *will* catch on—don't rescue them too early).
2. Sing "Who's That Knocking at My Window?" Say, "Sing with me," and sing the first part of the song with no visual aids: "Who's that knocking at my window? Who's that knocking at my door?" Near the end of the first part, pull out your sheets that have the pictures of two animals on them. Students sing the second part with you, naming the two animals: "Horses knocking at my window; Butterflies knocking at my door." After doing the animals you did in the last lesson, introduce one or two new sheets with new animals on them. Continue until you don't have any animal sheets left or students lose interest.
3. Lead Croc and Dog Dialogue. Take Croc out of your bag and say, "My crocodile is trying to learn to sing. Let's see how he does with 'Rain Rain Go Away.'" Have Croc *speak* "Rain, rain, go away." Ask, "Did Croc sing or speak it? Let's have him try again." Have Croc speak it again, but slightly louder (not better). Ask, "Did Croc sing it that time? Let's see if someone can help him."
4. The Dog Sings. Bring out Dog and have Dog sing in his singing voice at the appropriate pitch level. Ask, "Did Dog sing or speak it? He sang it! Croc, can you try singing it like Dog?" Have Dog model singing and have Croc slowly get slightly higher each time until he finally gets it. Cheer for the Croc and invite everyone to sing "Rain, Rain Go Away" with Croc since he finally got it.
5. Sing "Firefly." Say, "Sing with me," and sing the "Firefly" song, whispering "Goodnight firefly" at the end.

Extensions

1. Echo body percussion.
2. Ask them to tell you the things they did in music today: "Raise your hand if you can tell me one thing we did today."
3. Tell a story or sing a song for them.

16

Intermediate Elementary Lessons (Grades 2 and 3)

About Students in These Grades

You'll notice a difference in these children from your kindergarten and first grade students. Grades 2 and 3 generally include children who are 7, 8, or 9 years old. Many students in these grades are eager to learn, can read well, and are able to show greater independence and responsibility. These qualities can make for delightful music making for them and joyful teaching for you.

About These Lessons

Chapter 5 gives detailed steps for preparing to teach these lessons. I will just remind you to put time into practicing your lessons; know them so well that you can improvise when things don't go as expected. And remember that each part of the lesson should take between 5 and 7 minutes—don't spend too long on one thing.

All of the lessons have been designed so that you can deliver them without additional resources. I recommend using a presentation program like PowerPoint or Google Slides to simplify your visual aids and speed up your preparation. Otherwise, use posterboard and markers to make large visual aids that all of your students will be able to see.

I used the Takadimi rhythm counting system in these lessons. I think this is a great system for all levels of music teaching, but you are welcome to use a different system. I do not, however, recommend using a system in which you count the meter (e.g., "one-e-and-a two-and three-and-a" or "one-ta-tay-ta two-tay three-la-li") because these systems require an additional step of understanding meter, rather than just understanding the number of sounds on a beat. See Chapter 13 for a fuller discussion of this.

Your First Year as an Elementary Music Teacher. Andrew S. Paney, Oxford University Press. © Oxford University Press 2025.
DOI: 10.1093/oso/9780197631430.003.0016

Lesson 1: Setting the Tone

This first lesson can help to set the tone for the year. Anticipate a joyful, orderly, musical experience with your students.

Objectives. Students will:

- Demonstrate classroom procedures (rules, seating charts).
- Create arrangements of a rhyme with body percussion.
- Notate sounds using icons.
- Perform their creations for a small group.
- Listen to contrasting music selections.

Materials

- Your filled-in seating chart. (See ▶ Visual 3.1 and Chapter 3 for information on how to create one).
- A poster with your class expectations. See ▶ Visual 15.2 (See Chapter 4 for more about expectations).
- Projected or handwritten, large visual of the text of "Queen, Queen Caroline" printed neatly, by hand, on the board, with space between each line.
- Copies of "Queen, Queen Caroline," one for each student, See ▶Visual 16.1.
- A pitch instrument (piano, tuning fork, or an app on your phone).
- A medium or large, good-quality speaker.
- Elmo Document Camera or other opaque projector (optional).

Songs and Other Music

- "Queen, Queen Caroline" rhyme[1] (all songs and rhymes are printed in Appendix B).
- Recording of Bach, *Goldberg Variations*, Variation 5.[2]
- Recording of "ABC" by The Jackson 5.[3]

National Standards

- MU:Pr4.2.2.a—Demonstrate knowledge of music concepts (such as tonality and meter) in music from a variety of cultures selected for performance.
- MU:Re7.1.3.a—Demonstrate and describe how selected music connects to and is influenced by specific interests, experiences, or purposes.

Procedures

Hello (Opening Activities): Rhythm Echo and Getting Settled

1. Students enter. As students walk into your room, ask them to sit in any chair, or, if possible, have them sit or stand in an open space in your room.
2. Body Percussion. Say, "Echo me," and immediately clap a 4-beat pattern. Repeat with several patterns, getting slightly more difficult as you go. You can increase difficulty by

changing the tempo, the length of patterns, and which body percussion elements you use (snaps, claps, pats, and stomps).

Learn 1 (Primary Learning Objective): Classroom Procedures

1. Introduction. Tell the students your name and help them pronounce it. Tell them one or two things about you that you care about (for example, I love to ride my bike, I read books on the beach, my dog chews on my furniture and I love her, etc.). The more unique and funny, the better! You can include photos in your slides (or even show printed photos) to help them understand who you are.
2. Seating chart. Walk to a seat and say the name of the student you have assigned to sit there. Move to the next seat and invite the next student to sit there. Continue until all children are in their assigned seats. Note who is absent from the vacancies in your seating chart.
3. Classroom procedures for entering music class. I suggest, "In music class we walk carefully and quietly. Each time you come to music class, please walk quietly to your assigned seat. Let's practice it now." Ask for two or three volunteers to line up just outside the room or near the door and to practice their entry. Repeat as many times as necessary to have a successful entry. They will enjoy the challenge of meeting your high standard!
4. Classroom expectations. Walk them through each of your expectations (▶Visual 15.2 has the following: "Show Respect," "Follow Directions," and "Do Your Best"—see Chapter 4 for more about this).

Wildcard (Change of Pace): Group Quiz

1. Quick Group Quiz. Ask your students some questions about the expectations and procedures for class. Do this orally and have students raise their hands before answering (to show respect to you and to their classmates).
2. Use some scenarios, too: "What expectations would you follow if you walked into music class one day and you had a substitute teacher?" "What can you do if you really want to play a particular instrument, but it feels like you never get chosen? What expectations can you remind yourself of?"

Learn 2 (Secondary Learning Objective): Composing with a Rhyme

1. "Queen, Queen Caroline"
   a) Teach the rhyme by rote. Say, "listen" and say the rhyme, "Queen, Queen Caroline" for them with expression and making lots of eye contact throughout the room. Ask questions about the rhyme to check understanding. Say, "Listen again," and say the rhyme again. Say, "Say it with me as softly as you can." Repeat the rhyme together more times until they know it well, varying it a little each time (louder or softer, higher pitch or lower, faster or slower, etc.)
   b) Show the text of the rhyme on the board or screen.

2. Write a class composition together.
   a) Say, "Let's add some symbols for body percussion. What could we add for claps?" In my model I use $ for stomps, # for pats, X for claps, and ^ for snaps. Each class will do it differently.

"Queen, Queen Caroline"

```
$     $     # # #
Queen, Queen Caroline
                X X X
Washed her hair in turpentine
X   X   X           ^
Turpentine to make it shine
$     $     # # #
Queen, Queen Caroline
```

   b) Ask, "Which word do think is most important in this rhyme?" Students may give you several answers. Choose one and ask, "What shall we do on that word: snap, clap, or pat?" Say the rhyme together, adding the body percussion they chose. Repeat this step with another important word.
   c) Create your Key. As you go or at the end of your composition, create a Key together. Here is mine:

Key

$	stomp
#	pat
X	clap
^	snap

   d) Students compose. Pass out papers with the rhyme text printed on it (▶ Visual 16.1), enough for each child to have one. Invite them to write their own version, like the one you did together. Ask them to use the same symbols you created as a class on their papers, and to write a Key on their papers, just like the one you created together on the board.
   e) Share compositions with classmates. Pair students up and ask them to do both of their compositions together. Students may notice that they need to clarify where their symbols are. They may also change some things based on their partner's ideas. This is great practice!

f) Share compositions with the class. Ask if anyone would like to share theirs with the class. Ask the pair to do the composition for the class together. Or, if you have a way to show their composition to the whole class in an appropriately large size (for example, an Elmo document camera or other opaque projector), read their compositions together. Repeat for as many minutes as you have left in the class, allowing 5 to 7 minutes for your closing activities.

g) Collect students' work or ask them to take them home.

Goodbye (Closing Activities): Undirected Listening

1. Listening. Say, "We will end our time together listening to two short pieces of music. There are a few things I need from you to help you and everyone else enjoy the music." Teach your expectations for listening times with your students. I use the following:

   Take a deep breath and relax in your seat.

   Keep your body and your mouth quiet.

   Listen to understand and enjoy.
2. Without any introduction, play two very short, contrasting listening examples. I suggest the following selections:
   a) Recording of Bach, *Goldberg Variations*, Variation 5
   b) Recording of "ABC" by The Jackson 5
3. Ask students about what they heard. After hearing both, ask them to turn and talk about the music, starting with a general question like: What did you hear in those two pieces? Invite them to turn and ask someone next to them for their thoughts and to tell them theirs. If they don't talk much, ask more direct questions: What was making the sounds? Can they name any of the instruments? Was there singing? Did it sound like more than one person was making music at the same time? Can someone hum a part of the first one? The second one? What emotions do you think this music is expressing? What emotions did you feel while listening?
4. Dismiss them to line up at the door, one row at a time.

Extension

If you need to fill more time, dismiss them one student at a time and ask each student to answer a simple question as you call their name: "Do you prefer ice cream or cake?" Or "Do you prefer walking or biking?" If you'd like this to be a quiet time, ask them to give a sign as they leave, for instance, "Raise your hand if you choose walking or raise two hands if you prefer biking." See Chapter 12 for more ideas for ending class.

Lesson 2: Building Excitement

A lot of your second lesson will be similar to the first lesson. You are building on the procedures and activities you did in the first class. As with every music lesson, give your students space to have a joyful, orderly, musical experience.

Objectives. Students will:

- Practice and explain classroom procedures (rules, seating charts).
- Sing short songs.
- Arrange songs with body percussion.
- Play and compose with instruments.
- Practice and perform their compositions for a small audience.
- Listen to and describe contrasting music.

Materials

- Your seating chart.
- Quick Quiz (▶ Visual 16.2) Review of Day 1.
- Visual aids of bread roll, lamb, and bridge (▶ Visual 16.3).
- Paper with the text of each of the songs, "Hot Cross Buns," "London Bridge Is Falling Down," and "Mary Had a Little Lamb" (▶ Visual 16.4).
- Recordings of listening examples.
- A medium or large, good-quality speaker.
- Markerboard, dry-erase markers, and eraser.
- Classroom set of pencils or pens.
- A pitch instrument (piano, tuning fork, or an app on your phone).

Songs and Other Music

- "Hot Cross Buns" song[4] (all songs and rhymes are printed in Appendix B).
- "Mary Had a Little Lamb" song.[5]
- "London Bridge Is Falling Down" song.[6]
- Recording of Bach, *Goldberg Variations*, Variation 5.
- Recording of "ABC" by The Jackson 5.

National Standards

- MU:Pr4.1.2.a—Demonstrate and explain personal interest in, knowledge about, and purpose of varied musical selections.
- MU:Pr4.2.3.b—When analyzing selected music, read and perform rhythmic patterns and melodic phrases using iconic and standard notation.

Procedures

Hello (Opening Activities): Rhythm Echo and Getting Settled

1. Students enter. Remind students in a soft voice to enter quietly and walk to their seats. Help students who were not present on the first day to find their assigned seats. If they enter loudly and cannot hear you, start with echo clapping: Say "Echo me," and clap patterns until everyone is following you and not talking. Then continue with your plan.

2. Double check the seating chart and learn names. Go around the room and say the name of each student. Invite them to correct your pronunciation (and take notes on your seating chart). Help them find the right seat if they're in the wrong spot.
3. Body Percussion. Say, "Echo me," and immediately clap a 4-beat pattern. Repeat with several patterns, getting slightly more difficult as you go.

Learn 1 (Primary Learning Objective): First Rhythm Lesson

1. Note that this lesson is included in Chapter 13, "Rhythm Lesson #1," too. I think it is a great way to introduce rhythm notation to older students quickly.
2. Say, "Echo me," and clap 4-beat patterns that include only ♩ and ♫. For example, you might clap ♩ ♩ ♩ ♩, ♩ ♩ ♩ ♫, ♩ ♩ ♫ ♩, or ♩ ♩ ♫ ♫. Students echo each 4-beat pattern you clap.
3. After completing several (7–10) patterns, clap this pattern: ♩ ♩ ♫ ♩ Repeat the same pattern after they echo. Without clapping it again, say, "Clap that pattern again, please."
4. After they clap, ask, "Which of these do you think represents that pattern?" Show them the following patterns on the board: ♩ ♩ ♩ ♩ and ♩ ♩ ♫ ♩.
   When they answer, ask them why they chose that one.
5. Point to the quarter note and say, "That's right! In music, this symbol stands for one sound on a beat and we call it '*ta*.' Can you find any other *ta*s?"
6. Point to the pair of eighth notes and say, "This other symbol stands for two sounds on one beat and we call it '*tadi*.' You would read this pattern '*ta ta tadi ta*.' Read it for me." Students read it aloud.
7. Try other patterns, too. "How would you read this one?" ♩ ♩ ♫ ♫ "What about this?" ♩ ♩ ♩ ♫ Students read other patterns. Continue to give different 4-beat patterns that use exclusively those two rhythms (♩ and ♫) while students read them.
8. Have students read several flashcards that use only *ta* and *tadi*, see "Flashcards 1: Just Read" in Chapter 13.

Wildcard (Change of Pace): Rhythm in Feet

1. Say, "Let's put the rhythm for these in our feet."
2. Students read a rhythm card with *ta*s and *tadi*s, then immediately step that rhythm with their feet, moving around the room.

Learn 2 (Secondary Learning Objective): Singing and Creating with a Melody

1. Mystery songs.
   - Show students three pictures (▶ Visual 16.3): a bread roll, a lamb, and a bridge. Say, "I'm going to tap the rhythm of a song and I want you to see if you can figure out which song it is. I've put some clues on the board that may help if you've already heard one or more of these songs." Tap the rhythm of one of the songs and say, "Show me with your fingers which song you think that is, song one, song two,

or song three." Acknowledge their answers without giving away the answer: "I see several people who think it's number three and a few who think number two." Repeat for the next two songs.

2. Teach the songs by rote.
   - Choose the song that most children know, based on your observations from the previous step. Reveal the answer by singing the song while you tap the rhythm. Sing it expressively and as though you enjoy the song, not just that you can sing it correctly.
   - Invite students to sing it with you: "Sing it with me as softly as you can." Having them sing softly allows students who don't yet know the song to hear you better and to have a more consistent model of the song. I encourage you to teach this by rote and not by reading. This will help develop your students' listening skills.
   - Repeat. Follow the same steps with the second and third songs. You will want to repeat the singing at least three times for each song to help those for whom the songs are new. Each time you repeat aim to add some element of interest: a slightly faster or slower tempo, a slightly louder or softer dynamic level, or add patting or snapping on the beat (clapping can get too loud with a class of 20–30).
3. Rebuild the class composition from the previous lesson together on the board or screen. Students create the key and body percussion.
4. Introduce four instruments. Choose unpitched percussion classroom instruments that you have multiples of (e.g., rhythm sticks, maracas, etc.). Tell students the name of each and how to play it.
5. Pass out instruments. Choose one of the four instruments and ask the class to name that instrument. Show students how you'd like them to hold it so that the instrument is quiet when it's not being played. After passing instruments out, students replace each body percussion part in the class creation with one of the instruments. Ask them to consider the sound of the instrument and how it will fit the text and character of the rhyme.
6. Update your key to show the body percussion and the instrument parts. See example.
7. Ask students to perform the rhyme in multiple ways: saying the rhyme with body percussion, saying the rhyme with instruments, instruments alone with inner hearing of the rhyme, etc. Then have them perform their compositions in small groups of four or five. Invite students to share them with the class if time allows.

Goodbye (Closing Activities): Undirected Listening

1. Set up listening. Students have just experienced listening as an audience, but it won't hurt to remind them of your expectations for listening times with your students (Take a deep breath and relax in your seat; Keep your body and your mouth quiet; Listen to understand and enjoy).
2. Students listen. Play the same two very short, contrasting listening examples that you played in the previous lesson (Bach and Jackson 5). Again, avoid setting up or introducing the music, just let them enjoy the experience.

3. Students share. After hearing both, ask them to turn and talk about the music, starting with a general question like: What did you notice about these pieces? What did you notice that you missed last time we met? As time allows, ask them if any of their answers changed to these questions you asked yesterday.
4. Dismiss them to line up at the door, one row at a time.

Extension

If you need to fill more time, repeat the echo clapping activity from the beginning of class. You can add interest by also including pats, snaps, or stomps. Consider allowing a student to lead, too.

Lesson 3: Giving Ownership

In this lesson you'll build on the things you've done so far and give students choices to exercise their artistry, their creativity. You'll keep it an orderly, enjoyable experience for all by reinforcing classroom expectations and keeping tasks moving at a good pace.

Objectives. Students will:

- Read and perform rhythms ta and tadi.
- Create and perform with singing and body percussion.
- Play and compose with instruments.
- Practice and perform their compositions for a small audience.
- Evaluate and modify their compositions.
- Listen to and describe contrasting music.

Materials

- Your seating chart.
- Rhythm Flashcards. Make them or use ▶Visual 16.5.
- Students' work from the previous class on ▶Visual 16.4, and extra blank copies for students who were absent.
- Crossword Puzzle. ▶Visual 16.6.
- Recordings of listening examples.
- Visual aid of the names of the two listening examples. ▶Visual 16.7.
- A medium or large, good-quality speaker.
- Markerboard, dry-erase markers, and eraser.
- Classroom set of pencils or pens.
- A pitch instrument (piano, tuning fork, or an app on your phone).

Songs and Other Music

- "Queen, Queen Caroline" rhyme.
- "Hot Cross Buns" song.

- "London Bridge Is Falling Down" song.
- "Mary Had a Little Lamb" song.
- Recording of Bach, *Goldberg Variations,* Variation 5.
- Recording of "ABC" by The Jackson 5.

National Standards

- MU:Re7.1.2.a—Explain and demonstrate how personal interests and experiences influence musical selection for specific purposes.
- MU:Pr4.1.3.a—Demonstrate and explain how the selection of music to perform is influenced by personal interest, knowledge, purpose, and context.

Procedures

Hello

1. Say, "Echo me," and clap several patterns, using only *ta* and *tadi.*
2. Continue to echo patterns, but instead of clapping, say rhythm syllables: "*ta ta tadi ta,*" "*tadi tadi ta ta.*" Do this about three to five times before proceeding to the next step.
3. Show students a large flashcard (▶Visual 16.5 or create your own that are at least 11 inches by 4.25 inches, a half sheet of printer paper) with four beats of notation and including *only* known rhythms: *ta* and *tadi.*
4. Ask them to read each. Count, "One, two, three, four," and have them say the rhythm. Do not say the rhythm with them. If you point to what they're reading, only point to the beats, not the rhythms—they need to be making their rhythms match your beat.

Learn 1

1. Write the rhythm of one of your songs that only has *ta*s and *tadi*s in it on the board (see Figure 16.1 for a model):
2. Ask students to read those rhythms aloud, using rhythm syllables (*ta*s and *tadi*s).
3. Say something like, "We've sung a song with this rhythm in class. Can you figure out which one it is?" Once students know the song (either by figuring it out or by you revealing the answer), sing the song together (my example is "Mary Had a Little Lamb").
4. Introduce the task today: "Today we will take your compositions and record them. But first we need to remember our rhymes and songs. Sing with me."
5. Review learned music. Sing all of the songs and rhymes you've done so far together: "Hot Cross Buns," "London Bridge Is Falling Down," "Queen, Queen Caroline," and "Mary Had a Little Lamb." Help them if they need help and repeat the songs with which they struggle.
6. Return their work from last class. Ask students to return to their groups from the previous music class. Pass out the papers they submitted last week. If these have been misplaced, just have them create them again right away (you will need to have some extra copies available of ▶Visual 16.4).

FIGURE 16.1 Mystery song. Write this rhythm (or another one) and ask students to read it in their heads and figure out what is.

7. Give them a goal. Tell students that later in the class you will be audio-recording them performing their compositions.
8. Students practice. Ask the groups to choose one of their pieces and to practice it. Allow them to change and develop their compositions if they'd like to.

Wildcard

1. As groups finish their practice, pass out Crossword Puzzle (▶ Visual 16.6). This wildcard activity allows for groups who move more slowly (or more quickly) with their compositions to have the time they need without feeling rushed or sitting idly.
2. Students who finish the crossword early may draw on the back of it.

Learn 2

1. As students finish the crossword and their practice, ask them to sign up for a slot on the board. This will be the "set list" when you begin recording.
2. When you feel like the practice and crossword time has finished (probably between 10 and 15 minutes), bring everyone back together, show them the "set list," and tell them there are important steps every single one of them will have to do to make this work.
3. First, remind students of appropriate audience etiquette: We listen with interest and excitement. We keep our mouths and bodies quiet. We clap when they finish.

4. Second, talk about what kind of silence they will need to achieve to have good recordings. Give examples of rustling papers, kicking feet, and sniffles and coughs. Ask them to be perfectly quiet for 10 seconds and stop them each time you hear even the faintest sound. Try it again until you are successful.
5. It's time to record! I recommend doing only an audio recording, not a video recording. This allows them to focus on the sounds they're making rather than what they look like. Have the first group on the "set list" perform their piece while others practice being a good audience. Stop the recording when they finish.
6. Repeat for each group.
7. If you have time, listen to all of the recordings together.

Goodbye: Undirected Listening

1. To end class, Show students the names of the two pieces you've played for them at each class period so far, on ▶ Visual 16.7. Ask them which of the pieces they'd like to hear first. Play their choice first, then the other selection.
2. Say, "I'm going to change the music next time I see you. Is there one of these you'd like me to keep in my plan?" Allow students to respond and to tell why they want to keep a particular piece.
3. Dismiss students to line up at the door.

Extension

If you need more time, ask students which of the songs or rhymes they'd like to do again as they line up. Find ways to vary their choice, if necessary: faster and slower, louder and softer, higher and lower, while patting the beat and while clapping the rhythm, etc. If you run out of ideas, ask them to help you think of more!

17

Older Elementary Lessons (Grades 4 Through 6)

About Students in These Grades

Grades 4, 5, and 6 include children who are 9, 10, 11, and 12 years old, generally. These students are often able to do many things independently and enjoy creating and performing. They also start to become more aware of themselves and of their peers. This can make it slightly more difficult for the teacher, as they may react as though some activities are too young for them or not "cool" enough. With a good start, though, you will love working with these students. You will win them over and they will eagerly anticipate coming to music class.

There are big differences between kids who are 7 and those who are 12. But there are some significant similarities, too, including that these students generally know how to read and have experienced schooling for more than just a year or two. These similarities allow for similarities in your lesson plans.

In this chapter, you'll see that I've suggested that you teach a lesson extremely similar to the lessons written for grades 2 and 3. The only difference is the rhyme choice ("Bate, Bate Chocolate" instead of "Queen, Queen Caroline") and the additional ways to extend a lesson. I don't usually teach the same lesson to different grades, and I don't expect you to, either. But in this case, I think it is a benefit for you with little or no cost to your students. You will be able to spend more time preparing fewer lessons. You also will see the differences in how these ages approach tasks and solve problems. They have differences in their physical, mental, and even emotional development. Your younger and older students will *not* give you the same responses, though you will be giving them similar experiences.

Some classes will move more quickly than others. In these plans, I've included optional additional activities ("If Time Allows" headings) with more variations, more freedom for students, and more ways for them to express themselves with greater responsibility.

Your First Year as an Elementary Music Teacher. Andrew S. Paney, Oxford University Press. © Oxford University Press 2025.
DOI: 10.1093/oso/9780197631430.003.0017

About These Lessons

You read the detailed steps for preparing to teach these lessons in Chapter 5. Here, I will just remind you to practice your lessons; know them so well that you can improvise when things don't go as expected. And remember that each part of the lesson should take between 5 and 7 minutes—don't spend too long on one thing.

All of the lessons have been designed so that you can deliver them without additional resources. But if you can, I suggest using PowerPoint or Google Slides to simplify your visual aids and speed up your preparation.

I chose to use the Takadimi rhythm counting system in these lessons. See Chapter 13 for a fuller discussion of rhythm counting systems.

Lesson 1: Setting the Tone

This first lesson can help to set the tone for the year. Anticipate a joyful, orderly, musical experience with your students.

Objectives. Students will:

- Demonstrate classroom procedures (rules, seating charts).
- Create arrangements of a rhyme with body percussion.
- Notate sounds using icons.
- Perform their creations for a small group.
- Listen to contrasting music selections.

Materials

- Your filled-in seating chart. (See ▶ Visual 3.1 and Chapter 3 for information on how to create one.)
- A poster with your class expectations. (▶ Visual 15.2. See Chapter 4 for more about expectations.)
- Projected or handwritten, large visual of the text of "Bate, Bate Chocolate" printed neatly, by hand, on the board, with space between each line.
- Copies of "Bate, Bate Chocolate," one for each student (▶ Visual 17.1).
- A pitch instrument (piano, tuning fork, or an app on your phone).
- A medium or large, good-quality speaker.
- Elmo Document Camera or other opaque projector (optional).

Songs and Other Music

- "Bate, Bate Chocolate" rhyme[1] (all songs and rhymes are printed in Appendix B).
- Recording of Bach, *Goldberg Variations*, Variation 5.[2]
- Recording of "ABC" by The Jackson 5.[3]

National Standards

- MU:Cr3.1.4.a—Present the final version of personal created music to others, and explain connection to expressive intent.
- MU:Pr4.1.5.a—Demonstrate and explain how the selection of music to perform is influenced by personal interest, knowledge, and context, as well as their personal and others' technical skill.

Procedures

Hello (Opening Activities): Rhythm Echo and Getting Settled

1. Students enter. As students walk into your room, ask them to sit in any chair, or, if possible, have them sit or stand in an open space in your room.
2. Body Percussion. Say, "Echo me," and immediately clap a 4-beat pattern. Repeat with several patterns, getting slightly more difficult as you go. You can increase difficulty by changing the tempo, the length of patterns, and which body percussion elements you use (snaps, claps, pats, and stomps).

Learn 1 (Primary Learning Objective): Classroom Procedures

1. Introduction. Tell the students your name and help them pronounce it. Tell them one or two things about you that you care about (for example, I love to ride my bike, I read books on the beach, my dog chews on my furniture and I love her, etc.). The more unique and funnier, the better! You can include photos in your slides (or even show printed photos) to help them understand who you are.
2. Seating chart. Walk to a seat and say the name of the student you have assigned to sit there. Move to the next seat and invite the next student to sit there. Continue until all children are in their assigned seats. Note who is absent from the vacancies in your seating chart.
3. Classroom procedures for entering music class. I suggest, "In music class we walk carefully and quietly. Each time you come to music class, please walk quietly to your assigned seat. Let's practice it now." Ask for two or three volunteers to line up just outside the room or near the door and to practice their entry. Repeat as many times as necessary to have a successful entry. They will enjoy the challenge of meeting your high standard!
4. Classroom expectations. Walk them through each of your expectations (▶Visual 15.2).

Wildcard (Change of Pace): Group Quiz

1. Quick Group Quiz. Ask your students some questions about the expectations and procedures for class. Do this orally and have students raise their hands before answering (to show respect to you and to their classmates).
2. Use some scenarios, too: "What expectations would you follow if you walked into music class one day and you had a substitute teacher?" "What can you do if you really want to play a particular instrument, but it feels like you never get chosen? What expectations can you remind yourself of?"

Learn 2 (Secondary Learning Objective): Composing with a Rhyme

1. Teach the rhyme by rote. Say, "listen," and say the rhyme "Bate, Bate Chocolate" for them with expression and making lots of eye contact throughout the room. Ask questions about the rhyme to check understanding and invite students to translate it for you. Help them if they don't know. Say, "Listen again," and say the rhyme again. Say, "Say it with me as softly as you can." Repeat the rhyme together more times until they know it well, varying it a little each time (louder or softer, higher pitch or lower, faster or slower, etc.)
2. Show the text of the rhyme on the board or screen.
3. Write a class composition together. "Let's add some symbols for body percussion. What could we add for claps?" In my model I use $ for stomps, # for pats, X for claps, and ^ for snaps. Each class will do it differently.

Bate, Bate Chocolate

```
# #   # #  $  $  $  $
Bate, Bate Chocolate
#    # X     #   #  ^ ^
Con arroz y con tomate
# #   # #  $  $  $  $
Bate, Bate Chocolate
#    # X     #   #  ^ ^
Con arroz y con tomate

^ ^   ^     ^      ^
Uno, dos, tres, CHO,
^ ^   ^     ^    X
Uno, dos, tres, CO,
^ ^   ^     ^    #
Uno, dos, tres, LA,
^ ^   ^     ^    $
Uno, dos, tres, TE,
# #   # #  $  $  $  $
Bate, Bate Chocolate (4 times)[4]
```

4. Ask, "Which word do think is most important in this rhyme?" Students may give you several answers. Choose one and ask, "What shall we do on that word: snap, clap, or pat?" Say the rhyme together, adding the body percussion they chose. Repeat this step with another important word.

5. Create your Key. As you go or at the end of your composition, create a Key together. Here is mine:

Key

$	stomp
#	pat
X	clap
^	snap

6. Students compose. Pass out papers with the rhyme text printed on it (▶ Visual 17.1), enough for each child to have one. Invite them to write their own version, like the one you did together. Ask them to use the same symbols you created as a class on their papers, and to write a Key on their papers, just like the one you created together on the board.
7. Share compositions with classmates. Pair students up and ask them to do both of their compositions together. Students may notice that they need to clarify where their symbols are. They may also change some things based on their partner's ideas. This is great practice!
8. Share compositions with the class. Ask if anyone would like to share theirs with the class. Ask the pair to do the composition for the class together. Or, if you have a way to show their composition to the whole class in an appropriately large size (for example, an Elmo document camera or other opaque projector), read their compositions together. Repeat for as many minutes as you have left in the class, allowing 5 to 7 minutes for your closing activities.
9. Collect students' compositions or ask them to take them home.

Goodbye (Closing Activities): Undirected Listening

1. Listening. Say, "We will end our time together listening to two short pieces of music. There are a few things I need from you to help you and everyone else enjoy the music." Teach your expectations for listening times with your students. I use the following:

   Take a deep breath and relax in your seat.
   Keep your body and your mouth quiet.
   Listen to understand and enjoy.
2. Without any introduction, play two very short, contrasting listening examples. I suggest the following selections:
   - Recording of Bach, *Goldberg Variations*, Variation 5.
   - Recording of "ABC" by The Jackson 5.
3. Ask students about what they heard. After hearing both, ask them to talk about the music, starting with a general question like: What did you hear in those two pieces?

Invite them to turn and ask someone next to them for their thoughts and to tell them theirs. If they don't talk much, ask more direct questions: What was making the sounds? Can they name any of the instruments? Was there singing? Did it sound like more than one person was making music at the same time? Can someone hum a part of the first one? The second one? What emotions do you think this music is expressing? What emotions did you feel while listening?

4. Dismiss them to line up at the door, one row at a time.

Extension

If you need to fill more time, dismiss them one student at a time and ask each student to answer a simple question as you call their name: "Do you prefer ice cream or cake?" Or "Do you prefer walking or biking?" If you'd like this to be a quiet time, ask them to give a sign as they leave, for instance, "Raise your hand if you choose walking or raise two hands if you prefer biking." See Chapter 12 for more ideas for ending class.

Lesson 2: Building Excitement

A lot of your second lesson will be similar to the first lesson. You are building on the procedures and activities you did in the first class. As with every music lesson, give your students space to have a joyful, orderly, musical experience.

Objectives. Students will:

- Practice and explain classroom procedures (rules, seating charts).
- Sing short songs.
- Arrange songs with body percussion.
- Play and compose with instruments.
- Practice and perform their compositions for a small audience.
- Listen to and describe contrasting music.

Materials

- Your seating chart.
- Quick Quiz (▶ Visual 16.2) Review of Day 1.
- Pictures of bread roll, lamb, and bridge (▶ Visual 16.3).
- Paper with the text of each of the songs, "Hot Cross Buns," "London Bridge Is Falling Down," and "Mary Had a Little Lamb." (▶ Visual 16.4).
- Recordings of listening examples.
- A medium or large, good-quality speaker.
- Markerboard, dry-erase markers, and eraser.
- Classroom set of pencils or pens.
- A pitch instrument (piano, tuning fork, or an app on your phone).

- At least four different classroom instruments, enough so that each child can have one (not one of each). I suggest rhythm sticks, maracas, hand drums, and finger cymbals. You do not need the same number of each.

Songs and Other Music

- "Hot Cross Buns" song.[5]
- "Mary Had a Little Lamb" song.[6]
- "London Bridge Is Falling Down" song.[7]
- Recording of Bach, *Goldberg Variations*, Variation 5.
- Recording of "ABC" by The Jackson 5.

National Standards

- MU:Pr4.1.4.a—Demonstrate and explain how the selection of music to perform is influenced by personal interest, knowledge, context, and technical skill.
- MU:Re7.1.4.a—Demonstrate and explain how selected music connects to and is influenced by specific interests, experiences, purposes, or contexts.
- MU:Re7.1.5.a—Demonstrate and explain, citing evidence, how selected music connects to and is influenced by specific interests, experiences, purposes, or contexts.

Procedures

Hello (Opening Activities): Rhythm Echo and Getting Settled

1. Students enter. Remind students in a soft voice to enter quietly and walk to their seats. Help students who were not present on the first day to find their assigned seats. If they enter loudly and cannot hear you, start with echo clapping: Say "Echo me," and clap patterns until everyone is following you and not talking. Then continue with your plan.
2. Double check the seating chart and learn names. Go around the room and say the name of each student. Invite them to correct your pronunciation (and take notes on your seating chart). Help them find the right seat if they're in the wrong spot.
3. Body Percussion. Say, "Echo me," and immediately clap a 4-beat pattern. Repeat with several patterns, getting slightly more difficult as you go.

Learn 1 (Primary Learning Objective): First Rhythm Lesson

1. Note that this lesson is included in Chapter 13, "Rhythm Lesson #1," too. I think it is a great way to introduce rhythm notation to older students quickly.
2. Say, "Echo me," and clap 4-beat patterns that include only ♩ and ♫. For example, you might clap ♩ ♩ ♩ ♩, ♩ ♩ ♩ ♫, ♩ ♩ ♫ ♩, or ♩ ♩ ♫ ♫. Students echo each 4-beat pattern you clap.
3. After completing several (7–10) patterns, clap this pattern: ♩ ♩ ♫ ♩ Repeat the same pattern after they echo. Without clapping it again, say "Clap that pattern again, please."

4. After they clap, ask, "Which of these do you think represents that pattern?" Show them the following patterns on the board: ♩ ♩ ♩ ♩ and ♩ ♩ ♫ ♩.
   When they answer, ask them why they chose that one.
5. Point to the quarter note and say, "That's right! In music, this symbol stands for one sound on a beat and we call it '*ta.*' Can you find any other *tas*?"
6. Point to the pair of eighth notes and say, "This other symbol stands for two sounds on one beat and we call it '*tadi.*' You would read this pattern '*ta ta tadi ta.*' Read it for me." Students read it aloud.
7. Try other patterns, too. "How would you read this one?" ♩ ♩ ♫ ♫ "What about this?" ♩ ♩ ♩ ♫ Students read other patterns. Continue to give different 4-beat patterns that use exclusively those two rhythms (♩ and ♫) while students read them.
8. Have students read several flashcards that use only *ta* and *tad*i, see "Flashcards 1: Just Read" in Chapter 13.

Wildcard (Change of Pace): Class Quiz

1. Quick group quiz. Ask the questions on ▶ Visual 16.2 aloud and present them on your screen (if possible). Invite students to raise their hands to answer or to vote on their answer. This should be a quieter time for students, a break from the amount of sound you have already made together.

Learn 2 (Secondary Learning Objective): Singing and Creating with a Melody

1. Mystery songs. Show students three pictures (▶ Visual 16.3): a bread roll, a lamb, and a bridge. Say, "I'm going to tap the rhythm of a song and I want you to see if you can figure out which song it is. I've put some clues on the board that may help if you've already heard one or more of these songs." Tap the rhythm of one of the songs and say, "Show me with your fingers which song you think that is, song one, song two, or song three." Acknowledge their answers without giving away the answer: "I see several people who think it's number three and a few who think number two." Repeat for the next two songs.
2. Teach the songs by rote. Choose the song that most children know, based on your observations from the previous step. Reveal the answer by singing the song while you tap the rhythm. Sing it expressively and as though you enjoy the song, not just that you can sing it correctly. Invite students to sing it with you: "Sing it with me as softly as you can." Having them sing softly allows students who don't yet know the song to hear you better and to have a more consistent model of the song. I encourage you to teach this by rote and not by reading. This will help develop your students' listening skills.
3. Repeat. Follow the same steps with the second and third songs. You will want to repeat the singing at least three times for each song to help those for whom the songs are new. Each time you repeat aim to add some element of interest: a slightly faster or slower

tempo, a slightly louder or softer dynamic level, or add patting or snapping on the beat (clapping can get too loud with a class of 20–30).

If Time Allows

- Rebuild your class composition from your first lesson on the board. Ask students to recreate from memory the Key and the body percussion they added to your previous work. See the example for "Bate Bate" above.
- Introduce four instruments. Choose any four unpitched percussion classroom instruments that you have multiples of. I use rhythm sticks, maracas, hand drums, and finger cymbals. Tell students the name of each and how to play it.
- Pass out instruments. Choose one of the four instruments and ask the class the name of that instrument. Show students how you'd like them to hold the instrument so that it is quiet when they are not playing. Pass out just one instrument to one child and ask them to show you how to hold it quietly, then how to play it. Allow each child to choose one of the instruments, releasing them one or two at a time. You should have three to nine of each instrument. Be sure to keep the instruments grouped together so that students can follow others in their group.
- Ask students to replace each of the body percussion parts in "Bate, Bate Chocolate" with one of the instruments. Ask them to consider the sound of the instrument and how it will fit. Do this until each body percussion part also has an instrument part.
- Update your Key to show the body percussion and the instrument parts:

Key

$ stomp AND hand drum

pat AND maracas

X clap AND rhythm sticks

^ snap AND finger cymbals

- Perform multiple ways. Ask students to perform the rhyme in multiple ways: saying the rhyme with body percussion, saying the rhyme with instruments, instruments alone without saying the rhyme (but keeping the rhyme going internally), body percussion alone, saying the rhyme alone, etc.

Change of Pace

1. Assign Groups. Walk around the room and form groups of three or four students. Make sure students who were absent for the first day of class are in groups with at least two students who were there. Alternatively, if there are more than three students who were not present for the previous lesson, invite them to do the activity with you at the board. See Chapter 5 for suggestions on leading successful groupwork.
2. Students choose. Pass out a paper with the text of each of the three songs to every student. Ask them to choose one of the three songs.
3. Students analyze. Ask students to answer these questions in their groups: "Which words are most significant in this song?" "What do you want to do on those words: snap, clap, or pat or stomp?" Tell them to try their song in several different ways and to choose what their groups likes best.
4. Students write. Ask them to make a clean copy of their choices for where sounds should be and a key showing what sounds they are using.

If Time Allows

- Add instruments. If students finish early, ask them to add instruments to their key, just as you did together on the board. Tell them you won't have time to perform with instruments today, but they can make a plan for another music class period.
- Students practice. "All musicians practice their work. Play your composition three to five times, and aim to get better each time."
- Students perform for a small audience. Combine two groups and have each group perform for the other. This will be a noisy time! When all have completed their work, ask for a volunteer group to come to the front and perform their composition.
- Students become an audience. Before the first group performs, teach your class how to be an audience: We listen with interest and excitement. We keep our mouths and bodies quiet. We clap when they finish.
- Students perform for a slightly larger audience. Allow every group who wants to perform to have a chance. You may need to write a "set list" on the board to keep things moving!
- Collect students' work or ask them to take them home.

Goodbye (Closing Activities): Undirected Listening

1. Set up listening. Students have just experienced listening as an audience, but it won't hurt to remind them of your expectations for listening times with your students (Take a deep breath and relax in your seat; Keep your body and your mouth quiet; Listen to understand and enjoy).
2. Students listen. Play the same two very short, contrasting listening examples that you played in the previous lesson (Bach and Jackson 5). Again, avoid setting up or introducing the music, just let them enjoy the experience.
3. Students share. After hearing both, ask them to turn and talk about the music, starting with a general question like: What did you notice about these pieces? What did you notice that you missed last time we met? As time allows, ask them if any of their answers changed to these questions you asked yesterday.
4. Dismiss them to line up at the door, one row at a time.

Extension

If you need to fill more time, repeat the echo clapping activity from the beginning of class. You can add interest by also including pats, snaps, or stomps. Consider allowing a student to lead, too.

Lesson 3: Giving Ownership

In this lesson you'll build on the things you've done so far and give students choices to exercise their artistry, their creativity. You'll keep it an orderly, enjoyable experience for all by reinforcing classroom expectations and keeping tasks moving at a good pace.

Objectives. Students will:

- Read and perform rhythms ta and tadi.
- Create and perform with singing and body percussion.
- Play and compose with instruments.
- Practice and perform their compositions for a small audience.
- Evaluate and modify their compositions.
- Listen to and describe contrasting music.

Materials

- Your seating chart.
- Rhythm Flashcards. Make them or use ▶ Visual 16.5.
- Students' work from the previous class on ▶ Visual 16.4, and extra blank copies for students who were absent.
- Crossword Puzzle, ▶ Visual 16.6.
- Recordings of listening examples.

- Visual Aid of the names of the two listening examples. ▶ Visual 16.7.
- A medium or large, good-quality speaker.
- Markerboard, dry-erase markers, and eraser.
- Classroom set of pencils or pens.
- A pitch instrument (piano, tuning fork, or an app on your phone).
- At least four different classroom instruments, enough so that each child can have one (not one of each). I suggest rhythm sticks, maracas, hand drums, and finger cymbals. You do not need the same number of each.

Songs and Other Music

- "Bate, Bate Chocolate" rhyme.
- "Hot Cross Buns" song.
- "London Bridge Is Falling Down" song.
- "Mary Had a Little Lamb" song.
- Recording of Bach, *Goldberg Variations*, Variation 5.
- Recording of "ABC" by The Jackson 5.

National Standards

- MU:Pr4.2.4.b—When analyzing selected music, read and perform using iconic and/or standard notation.
- MU:Cr3.1.5.a—Present the final version of personal created music to others that demonstrates craftsmanship, and explain connection to expressive intent.
- MU:Pr4.2.5.b—When analyzing selected music, read and perform using standard notation.

Procedures

Hello

1. Say, "Echo me," and clap several patterns, using only *ta* and *tadi*.
2. Continue to echo patterns, but instead of clapping, say rhythm syllables: "*ta ta tadi ta*," "*tadi tadi ta ta*." Do this about three to five times before proceeding to the next step.
3. Show students a large flashcard (▶ Visual 16.5 or create your own that are at least 11 inches by 4.25 inches, a half sheet of printer paper) with four beats of notation and that includes *only* known rhythms: *ta* and *tadi*.
4. Ask them to read each. Count, "One, two, three, four," and have them say the rhythm. Do not say the rhythm with them. If you point to what they're reading, only point to the beats, not the rhythms—they need to be making their rhythms match your beat.

Learn 1

1. Write the rhythm of one of your songs that only has *ta*s and *tadi*s in it on the board (Figure 17.1):

FIGURE 17.1 Mystery song. Write this rhythm (or another one) and ask students to read it in their heads and figure out what is.

2. Ask students to read those rhythms aloud, using rhythm syllables (*tas* and *tadis*).
3. Say something like, "We've sung a song with this rhythm in class. Can you figure out which one it is?" Once students know the song (either by figuring it out or by you revealing the answer), sing the song together (my example is "Mary Had a Little Lamb").
4. Introduce the task today: "Today we will take your compositions and record them. But first we need to remember our rhymes and songs. Sing with me."
5. Review learned music. Sing all of the songs and rhymes you've done so far together: "Hot Cross Buns," "London Bridge Is Falling Down," "Bate, Bate Chocolate," and "Mary Had a Little Lamb." Help them if they need help and repeat the songs with which they struggle.

If Time Allows

- Rebuild your class composition from the previous lesson on the board. Ask students to recreate from memory the Key and the body percussion they added to your previous work. My example was:

Key

$ stomp AND hand drum
# pat AND maracas
X clap AND rhythm sticks
^ snap AND finger cymbals

Rhyme

```
 $          $  ###
Bate, Bate Chocolate
                  XXX
Con arroz y con tomate
X    X X          ^
Uno, dos, tres, CHO,
 $          $        ###
Bate, Bate Chocolate
```

- Add repetition and variation. Try different ways to repeat the rhyme with elements added or subtracted to make it interesting. Suggest an order yourself or ask students to choose one, for example:
  First, Say the rhyme.
  Second, Say the rhyme and do body percussion.
  Third, Say the rhyme and play instruments.
  Last, Instruments alone.
- Try it. Have the class perform the chosen order and evaluate and change if necessary. Ask them to go straight into the next repetition with no gap, keeping the beat continuously. This will make it a sharper, more interesting piece. Once they are happy with their performance, invite them to try it in their groups (see the following steps).

6. Return their work from last class. Ask students to return to their groups from the previous music class. Pass out the papers they submitted last week. If these have been misplaced, just have them create them again right away (you will need to have some extra copies available of ▶ Visual 16.4).
7. Give them a goal. Tell students that later in the class you will be audio-recording them performing their compositions.
8. Students practice. Ask the groups to choose one of their pieces and to practice it. Allow them to change and develop their compositions if they'd like to.

Wildcard

1. As groups finish their practice, pass out Crossword Puzzle (▶ Visual 16.6). This wildcard activity allows for groups who move more slowly (or more quickly) with their compositions to have the time they need without feeling rushed or sitting idly.
2. Students who finish the crossword early may draw on the back of it.

Learn 2

1. As students finish the crossword and their practice, ask them to sign up for a slot on the board. This will be the "set list" when you begin recording.
2. When you feel like the practice and crossword time has finished (probably between 10 and 15 minutes), bring everyone back together, show them the "set list," and tell them there are important steps every single one of them will have to do to make this work.
3. First, remind students of appropriate audience etiquette: We listen with interest and excitement. We keep our mouths and bodies quiet. We clap when they finish.
4. Second, talk about what kind of silence they will need to achieve to have good recordings. Give examples of rustling papers, kicking feet, and sniffles and coughs. Ask them to be perfectly quiet for 10 seconds and stop them each time you hear even the faintest sound. Try it again until you are successful.
5. It's time to record! I recommend doing only an audio recording, not a video recording. This allows them to focus on the sounds they're making rather than what they look like. Have the first group on the "set list" perform their piece while others practice being a good audience. Stop the recording when they finish.
6. Repeat for each group.
7. If you have time, listen to all of the recordings together.

Goodbye: Undirected Listening

1. To end class, Show students the names of the two pieces you've played for them at each class period so far, on ▶ Visual 16.7. Ask them which of the pieces they'd like to hear first. Play their choice first, then the other selection.
2. Say, "I'm going to change the music next time I see you. Is there one of these you'd like me to keep in my plan?" Allow students to respond and to tell why they want to keep a particular piece.
3. Dismiss students to line up at the door

Extension

If you need more time, ask students which of the songs or rhymes they'd like to do again as they line up. Find ways to vary their choice, if necessary: faster and slower, louder and softer, higher and lower, while patting the beat and while clapping the rhythm, etc. If you run out of ideas, ask them to help you think of more!

APPENDIX A

Visual Aids and Other Resources

3.1 Seating chart template.
15.1 "Listen and Sing" poster.
15.2 Classroom expectations poster: "Show Respect; Follow Directions; Do Your Best."
15.3 Picture of a cow.
15.4 Picture of an owl.
15.7 "Peas Porridge Hot" slides.
15.8 Body percussion composition cards.
15.9 Door and gate for "One Two Three Four, Mary at the Kitchen Door".
16.1 Text of "Queen, Queen Caroline".
16.2 Quick quiz, review of day 1.
16.3 Pictures of a bread roll, a lamb, and a bridge.
16.4 Texts of "Hot Cross Buns," "London Bridge Is Falling Down," and "Mary Had a Little Lamb".
16.5 Rhythm flashcards with ta and tadi.
16.6 Crossword puzzle.
16.7 Information about two listening examples.
17.1 Text of "Bate, Bate, Chocolate".

You may consult the above materials at the book's companion website: www.oup.com/us/YourFirstYearElementaryMusic

APPENDIX B

The Songs and Rhymes

A E I O U, La Vaca Eres Tu

Traditional

A E I O U
La vaca eres tú!

Note: I can't find this in a published source, but you can see it performed at the link above and if you search the title on youtube.com.

Bate, Bate Chocolate

Traditional

Bate, Bate Chocolate
Con arroz y con tomate.
Bate, Bate Chocolate
Con arroz y con tomate.

Uno, dos, tres, CHO
Uno, dos, tres, CO
Uno, dos, tres, LA
Uno, dos, tres, TE

Bate, Bate Chocolate
Bate, Bate Chocolate
Bate, Bate Chocolate
Bate, Bate Chocolate

"Bate, Bate Chocolate." (2022). In R. Gibson, *Canta Conmigo! Songs & Singing Games from Guatemala and Nicaragua* (p. 72). Oxford University Press.

Fishy, Fishy in the Brook

Traditional

Fishy, fishy in the brook
Daddy catch 'em with a hook.
Mama fry 'em in a pan.
Baby eat 'em like a man!

Public domain.

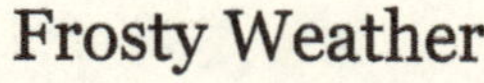

Frosty Weather

Traditional

Public domain.

Hot Crossed Buns

Traditional

Public domain.

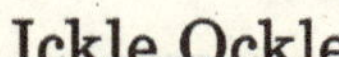

Ickle Ockle

Traditional

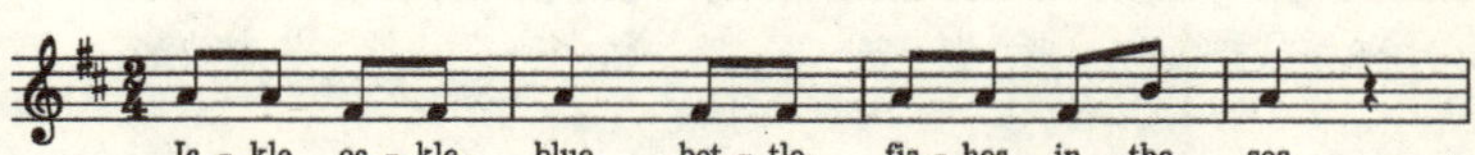

Public domain.

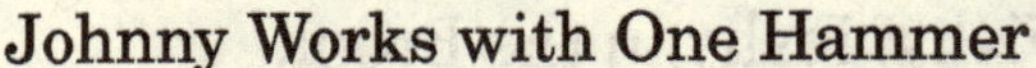

Johnny Works with One Hammer

Traditional

Public domain.

London Bridge

Traditional

Public domain.

Mary Had a Little Lamb

Traditional

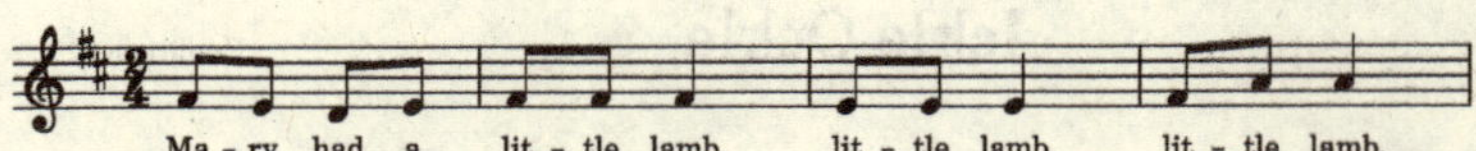

Public domain.

Mary at the Kitchen Door

Traditional

One Two Three Four
Mary at the kitchen door.
Five Six Seven Eight
Mary at the garden gate.

Public domain.

Peas Porridge Hot

Traditional

Peas porridge hot
Peas porridge cold
Peas porridge in a pot
Nine Days Old

Some like it hot
Some like it cold
Some like it in a pot
Nine Days Old

Queen, Queen Caroline

Traditional

Queen, Queen Caroline
Washed her hair in turpentine.
Turpentine to make it shine,
Queen, Queen Caroline.

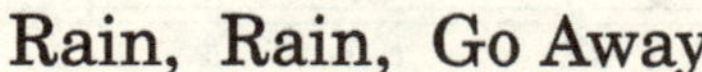

Traditional

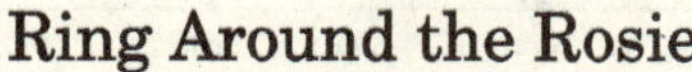

Traditional

Starlight

Traditional

Public domain.

Teddy Bear

Traditional

Public domain.

Who's that knocking?

Traditional

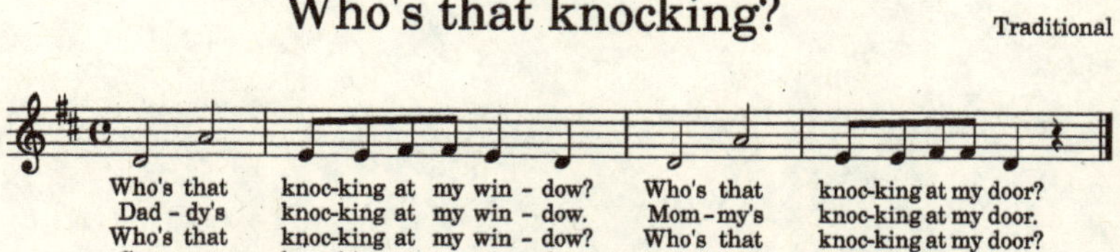

APPENDIX C

Outlined Lesson Plans

Early Elementary Lesson 1.
Early Elementary Lesson 2.
Early Elementary Lesson 3.
Intermediate Elementary Lesson 1.
Intermediate Elementary Lesson 2.
Intermediate Elementary Lesson 3.
Upper Elementary Lesson 1.
Upper Elementary Lesson 2.
Upper Elementary Lesson 3.

You may consult the above materials at the book's companion website: www.oup.com/us/YourFirstYearElementaryMusic

Notes

CHAPTER 2

1. See Gloria Ladson-Billings's many books on teaching students whose backgrounds differ from one's own, especially about culturally relevant pedagogy.

CHAPTER 3

1. Drawing marks on the floor may be discouraged at your school. Ask your friendly custodian if there would be a problem with drawing a small "L" to show where one leg of each chair should go. Marks on a tile floor will wear off within a year, even with permanent marker.
2. Create a space that works for all students, without making anyone feel like they don't fit. See articles and books on universal design. I recommend Darrow, A.-A. (2016). Applying the principles of universal design for learning in general music. In C. R. Abril & B. M. Gault (Eds.), *Teaching general music: Approaches, issues, and viewpoints* (pp. 308–326). Oxford University Press. https://doi.org/10.1093/acprof:oso/9780199328093.003.0015

CHAPTER 4

1. For an idea of the diversity of books on classroom management, see these titles: *Classroom management in the music room, Classroom management for elementary teachers: 15 Strategies to manage challenging behaviors and create a responsive classroom, Trauma-sensitive instruction: Creating a safe and predictable classroom environment, Classroom management for art, music, and PE teachers.*
2. This idea is supported by multiple studies. See Sieberer-Nagler, K. (2016). Effective classroom-management and positive teaching. *English Language Teaching*, 9(1), 163–172. http://dx.doi.org/10.5539/elt.v9n1p163

CHAPTER 5

1. I learned this list first from Dr. Susan Brumfield in my Kodály studies. You can find specific goals and objectives for students at any level at the NCAS website, https://www.nationalartsstandards.org/. Chapter 6 also addresses the NCAS in more detail.
2. I group these skills in four groups to aid my remembering of them: internal processing (listen, audiate, memorize), external processing (read, write, create), expressing (sing, play, move), and comparing (synthesize and contextualize).
3. Thanks to Janice Killian for pointing this out during a class I took with her in graduate school.

4. The development of this lesson format originated with the late Dr. Jean Ritchie. I learned it from her student, Dr. Susan Brumfield. There is a deeper explanation in her book. Brumfield, S. (2014). *First we sing! Kodály inspired teaching in the music classroom, a textbook for methodology*. Hal Leonard Publications.
5. Bee, bee, bumblebee. (2018). In S. Brumfield (Ed.), *First, we sing! 100 little songs and rhymes for reading, writing, and more! For primary grades* (p. 23). Hal Leonard.
6. Thanks to Sandy Knudson for this.

CHAPTER 6

1. Brumfield, S. (2014). *First we sing! Kodály inspired teaching in the music classroom, a textbook for methodology*. Hal Leonard. I took my Kodaly levels and wrote my dissertation with Susan and I highly recommend her teaching materials in the *First, We Sing* series. This particular idea may not be in the series, but it is a metaphor I like.
2. Brumfield, S. (Ed.). (2018). *First, we sing! 100 little songs and rhymes for reading, writing, and more! For primary grades*. Hal Leonard.
3. The first number identifies the Anchor Standard. The of the four practices has two or three Anchor Standards that are the same regardless of discipline and grade level. You can find more about these here: https://www.nationalartsstandards.org/
4. See Alice-Ann Darrow's excellent and brief article on universal design: Darrow, A.-A. (2010). Music education for all: Employing the principles of universal design to educational practice. *General Music Today, 24*(1), 43–45. https://doi.org/10.1177/1048371310376901

CHAPTER 7

1. See Waller-Pace, B. (2021). *Decolonizing the music room*. https://www.decolonizingthemusicroom.com/
2. Music Teacher Aileen Miracle addresses this in her excellent blogpost. Miracle, A. (2020). *Five songs I'm no longer using in my music room*. https://aileensmusicroom.com/2020/02/five-songs-im-no-longer-using-in-my-music-room.html
3. See also McDougle, L. (2023, July 31). *Songs with a questionable past*. https://docs.google.com/document/d/1q1jVGqOgKxfiUZ8N3oz0warXefGIJill2Xha-3X5nUY/preview

CHAPTER 8

1. Laskey, A., & Needleman, G. (n.d.). "Old MacDonald had a farm." *The American Folks Song Collection*. https://kodaly.hnu.edu/song.cfm?id=895
2. Waltz, R., & Engle, D. (Eds.). (2023). "To market, to market." *The traditional ballad index*. Retrieved October 31, 2023, from https://balladindex.org/Ballads/OO2339.html

CHAPTER 10

1. Robert Schumann wrote about caring for yourself as a musician, "When you have done your musical day's work and feel tired, do not exert yourself further. It is better to rest than to work without pleasure and vigour." Schumann, R. (1860). *Advice to young musicians* (H. H. Pierson, Trans.). J. Schuberth & Co. P. 12.

CHAPTER 12

1. "Tsuki (Firefly)." (2018). In S. Brumfield (Ed.), *First, we sing! 100 little songs and rhymes for reading, writing, and more! For primary grades* (p. 61). Hal Leonard.)

CHAPTER 15

1. "Who's that tapping at my window?" (2018). In S. Brumfield (Ed.), *First, we sing! 100 little songs and rhymes for reading, writing, and more! For primary grades* (p. 64). Hal Leonard.
2. Laskey, A. & Needleman, G. (n.d.). "Bluebells." *The American folks song collection*. https://kodaly.hnu.edu/song.cfm?id=459
3. "Ickle, ockle." (2018). In S. Brumfield (Ed.), *First, we sing! 100 little songs and rhymes for reading, writing, and more! For primary grades* (p. 32). Hal Leonard.

4. "Star light, star bright." (2018). In S. Brumfield (Ed.), *First, we sing! 100 little songs and rhymes for reading, writing, and more! For primary grades* (p. 58). Hal Leonard.
5. Waltz, R., & Engle, D. (Eds.). (n.d.). "One Two Three Four, Mary at the Cottage Door." *The traditional ballad index*. Retrieved January 15, 2023, from https://www.fresnostate.edu/folklore/ballads/CarMF077.html
6. "Frosty weather." (2018). In S. Brumfield (Ed.), *First, we sing! 100 little songs and rhymes for reading, writing, and more! For primary grades* (p. 23). Hal Leonard.
7. "Rain, rain, go away." (2018). In S. Brumfield (Ed.), *First, we sing! 100 little songs and rhymes for reading, writing, and more! For primary grades* (p. 53). Hal Leonard.

CHAPTER 16

1. "Queen, Queen Caroline." (2018). In S. Brumfield (Ed.), *First, we sing! 100 little songs and rhymes for reading, writing, and more! For primary grades* (p. 53). Hal Leonard.
2. Bach, J. S. (2013). Variatio 5. A 1 o vero 2 Clav. [Track recorded by Kimiko Ishizaka]. On *Bach: Goldberg Variations, BWV 988 (The Open Goldberg Variations)*. MuseScore.com
3. The Corporation. (1969). "ABC" [Song recorded by The Jackson 5]. On *ABC [Single]*.
4. "Hot cross buns." (2018). In S. Brumfield (Ed.), *First, we sing! 100 little songs and rhymes for reading, writing, and more! For primary grades* (p. 28). Hal Leonard.
5. Waltz, R., & Engle, D. (Eds.). (n.d.). "Mary had a little lamb." *The traditional ballad index*. Retrieved January 15, 2023, from https://www.fresnostate.edu/folklore/ballads/R360.html
6. "London bridge." (2018). In S. Brumfield (Ed.), *First, we sing! 100 little songs and rhymes for reading, writing, and more! For primary grades* (p. 38). Hal Leonard.

CHAPTER 17

1. "Bate, Bate Chocolate." (2022). In R. Gibson, *Canta Conmigo! Songs & Singing Games from Guatemala and Nicaragua* (p. 72). Oxford University Press.
2. Bach, J. S. (2013). Variatio 5. A 1 o vero 2 Clav. [Track recorded by Kimiko Ishizaka]. On *Bach: Goldberg Variations, BWV 988 (The Open Goldberg Variations)*. MuseScore.com
3. The Corporation. (1969). "ABC" [Song recorded by The Jackson 5]. On *ABC [Single]*.
4. Translation: Stir, stir the chocolate with rice and tomato. One, two, three CHO; one, two, three CO; one, two, three LA; one, two, three TE. Stir, stir the chocolate. Credit to Rachel Gibson for this translation.
5. Public Domain.
6. Public Domain.
7. Public Domain.

Index

For the benefit of digital users, indexed terms that span two pages (e.g., 52–53) may, on occasion, appear on only one of those pages.

Boxes are indicated by an italic *b* following the page number.